A RESOURCE GUIDE FOR TEACHERS & YOUTH MINISTERS

ACTIVITIES FOR CATHOLIC SOCIAL TEACHING

JAMES MCGINNIS

ave maria press  notre dame, indiana

As a Catholic educator and advocate for justice and peace since 1967, I am delighted to be able to bring these two strains of my life together in *Activities for Catholic Social Teaching*. I am grateful to the dedicated and visionary teachers I had in high school and the thousands of high school teachers I have worked with over the years. For this guide, I am especially grateful to those high school teachers and youth ministers who reviewed and/or tested these units. These include Kevin LaNave at the Center for Service Learning in St. Cloud, Minnesota; Rob Garavaglia at St. Louis University High School and Dan Darst at Christian Brothers High School in St. Louis; Dwyer Sullivan, Tim O'Connor, Chris Gutteridge, and Chris Reilly from St. Anne's and St. Michael Catholic Secondary Schools in Clinton and Stratford, Ontario; and Kathleen McGinnis, who for many years has taught Catholic high school students and college students preparing to teach high school social studies.

—James McGinnis

Founded in 1865, Ave Maria Press is a ministry of the Indiana Province of Holy Cross.

www.avemariapress.com

ISBN-10 1-59471-067-8 ISBN-13 978-1-59471-067-4

Cover and text design by John Carson

Printed and bound in the United States of America.

Contents

Introduction

Activities for Catholic Social Teaching: A Resource Guide for Teachers and Youth Ministers is intended to offer teenagers and those who work with them an informative, active, and reflective method of learning about Catholic social teaching. Designed around the chapters and themes of the textbook *Catholic Social Teaching: Learning and Living Justice* by Michael Pennock (Ave Maria Press, 2007), this guide offers directions for group and individual activities to facilitate this type of three-fold learning. The purpose of the book is to provide a collection of action-oriented assignments to enrich a high school theology course on Catholic social teaching or to encourage high school teens participating in parish youth ministry or religious education to delve more deeply into the rich body of information related to service of the poor and justice for all the world. Throughout this guide there will be several references to the *Catholic Social Teaching* Student Text.

The Methodology in This Resource: From Awareness to Concern to Action

Consistent with Catholic social teaching that is "action on behalf of justice and participation in the transformation of the world that fully appears to us to be a constitutive dimension of the preaching the Gospel" (*Justice in the World*, 1971), each chapter of this guide involves activities that lead students to *action*. However, to motivate students to action, there needs to be a component of *concern*, i.e., experiences that motivate students to action. And while the accompanying student text of *Catholic Social Teaching* provides most of the *awareness*, i.e., information about the issues, there are other awarenesses that are critical to this whole process of educating for peace and justice. All three components—awareness, concern, action—can be found somewhere in the activities in each chapter. In some cases, all three can be found within the same activity.

Affective resources and prayer

The activities address the "concern" component of the methodology through a variety of affective experiences—elements that touch students' hearts as well as their heads. These include stories, videos, songs, photos, role-plays, interviews, and other encounters with people. The prayerful reflections on Scripture, the prayer services, and the opportunities for silent prayer all help students hear in their hearts the call to peace and justice as a call from God.

Application

The "action" component of this methodology reflects a variety of action possibilities. Many activities invite students to apply the chapter theme to their personal lives, especially their relationships with classmates, friends, and family. Also, several activities encourage students to apply the theme of the chapter to their participation in their own community, nation, and world.

The action-reflection process

Most of the action suggestions are combined with opportunities for students to reflect on their experiences as a way of deepening the experience and integrating it more fully into their whole being. The student handout "Reflection on Personal Experiences" (Chapter 7, activity 1, page 126) is also appropriate for use with several other activities in this guide.

Diversity of learning styles

This resource tries to reflect the diversity of learning styles. Most of the activities involve reading, reflection, discussion, and sharing. But there are also several role-plays, art activities, poetry and musical elements, videos, interviews, and community research opportunities that reflect other learning styles and multiple intelligences.

Overview of the Chapters and Activities

Chapter 1—Catholic Social Teaching: An Overview

Activity 1 focuses on the principle of human dignity and provides a process for students to celebrate their own giftedness and that of their classmates.

Activity 2 focuses on service as our purpose in life, with Mother Teresa and Dr. Martin Luther King, Jr., as models.

Chapter 2—Justice and Virtues

Activity 1 presents the works of mercy and the works of justice as the two feet of Christian service and social action.

Activity 2 focuses on justice as participation and a redistribution of power and expressing it through class meetings.

Activity 3 explores God's justice in Scripture, from Exodus and Amos to Jesus and the early Church.

Activity 4 uses Micah 6:8 as the framework for living the virtues of justice and charity.

Chapter 3—Justice and Society

Activity 1 focuses on the realities of interdependence and the duty of solidarity.

Activity 2 applies the principle of the common good to family meetings and family service.

Activity 3 applies the common good to the "least" members of society.

Chapter 4—Justice and the Right to Life

Activity 1 explores the "seamless garment" and alternatives to abortion.

Activity 2 on euthanasia challenges students to be the compassion of God for those who are dying.

Activity 3 on capital punishment presents models of compassionate action for those on death row.

Chapter 5—Justice and Prejudice

Activity 1 focuses on students' own experiences of prejudice and discrimination.

Activity 2 challenges students to confront sexism in their lives.

Chapter 6—Justice and Racism

Activity 1 explores the realities of everyday racism and "white privilege."

Activity 2 encourages students to do their own "Racial Profile" and "Personal Affirmative Action" plan.

Activity 3 examines institutional racism and ways to confront it in local communities.

Activity 4 is a prayer service on responding to the sin of racism.

Chapter 7—Justice and Poverty

Activity 1 explores the realities of poverty and models of meeting and listening to the poor.

Activity 2 explores the impact of consumerism on our lives and how to challenge it.

Activity 3 challenges students to make a "preferential option for the poor."

Chapter 8—Justice and Peace

Activity 1 explores Jesus' way of peacemaking and its implications for his followers.

Activity 2 presents the "Youth Pledge of Nonviolence" as a way of responding to escalating violence.

Activity 3 focuses on forgiveness as the way to break the cycle of violence.

Activity 4 challenges students to be patriotic peacemakers, with Dr. Martin Luther King, Jr., as a model.

Chapter 9—Justice and Work

Activity 1 focuses on child labor and the "Free the Children" campaign.
Activity 2 presents an engaging case study about whether or not to cross a picket line.
Activity 3 explores a "just wage" and the importance of money for students.
Activity 4 explores students' attitudes toward work and workers.

Chapter 10—Justice and the Environment

Activity 1 presents twelve ways for growing in friendship with the earth as the basis for life-long stewardship.
Activity 2 offers a uniquely engaging process for becoming a prophet for God's creation.
Activity 3 provides opportunities for students to find God in creation and concludes with a "Litany of Repentance."

Additional Notes to Teachers

Optional elements and flexibility

Many of the activities identify optional elements to accommodate the amount of time you have for any one activity or chapter. Other activities may also require more time than a typical class session or youth meeting. Feel free to scale down, modify, or omit some of the steps, reflection/discussion questions, or student handouts identified in any of the activities.

Personal reflection

To encourage more thoughtful sharing, most of the handouts invite students to reflect silently and in writing before discussing issues. While this is important, it might be difficult for some students, especially extroverts who prefer to think aloud. You know your students. Vary the instructions to best serve the styles or the individuals you work with.

Discussions

To ensure that all students have a chance to think through and share their reflections or opinions, have students share in groups of two or three, or occasionally in somewhat larger groups, before whole class discussions. But don't be a slave to this process. Find out what works best for your group and go with your own mix of group sizes.

Affective elements

While it is explicitly pointed out in Chapter 10, there are other activities that may be difficult for some students to relate to for several reasons. First, they ask students to be vulnerable in front of their peers. You might acknowledge this ahead of time and invite students to take these risks, perhaps even praying together for the grace to do so. Whatever you can do to build up the level of trust in your group will make a real difference. Also, some students are more comfortable with the more traditional format of listen, take notes, discuss. Acknowledge ahead of time that a certain activity may make some of them uncomfortable, but that it is precisely the kind of activity through which other students learn best. Then encourage students to be open to different approaches.

Chapter 1

Catholic Social Teaching: An Overview

(See pages 9–27 of *Catholic Social Teaching*)

Catholic social teaching is summarized into some basic principles: an affirmation of the fundamental dignity of people, a call to respect all human life, and the call to family and community. In addition, those basic principles promote human rights and responsibilities, a preferential option for the poor and vulnerable, and the dignity of the work and workers. Finally, they call all people to work to achieve the common good, to live in solidarity with others, and to be good stewards of God's creation. These principles are expressed in the chapters of this book through particular activities.

Chapter 1, Activity 1

You Are God's Work of Art in Progress

Step 1—Introduction

Having high self-esteem and building up the self-esteem of others are important dimensions of putting Catholic social teaching into practice. There are ways of enhancing the dignity of every human being, which is the foundation of Catholic social teaching. They are also the foundation of working for justice and peace. It is difficult to care about others, to take risks for others, to rise above negative peer pressure unless we feel good about ourselves.

This activity is designed to help students experience their own dignity and that of their classmates through prayerful reflection and hands-on affirmation exercises. Depending on the length of your class periods, this activity might best be done in two classes, ending the first class with step 3 and asking students to do step 4 as their homework.

Step 2—Initial reflection on their own dignity

Discussion of photos

Ask students to bring a picture of something that they consider to be great art or the piece of art itself, plus a photo of themselves. You might supplement their pictures with pictures of widely acknowledged pieces of great art, e.g., Michelangelo's *David*, or *Pietá*. Discuss the comparative value of the two types of art—the artists' creations in marble and paint, and God's creation of human beings.

Reflection and sharing

Ask students to reflect on the phrase "You are God's work of art in progress" and what it means to them, perhaps sharing their thoughts with the whole class. You might conclude this exercise with these words:

> *What an incredible dignity we have! All who see the sculptures of Michelangelo are awed, especially by the* Pietà *and his* David. *But even the most beautiful and priceless piece of marble cannot compare to the beauty and value of a single human being. What a shame we don't sense our awesomeness each day.*

Step 3—What others say about our incredible dignity

What God says about us in Scripture

Distribute the student handout "You Are God's Work of Art in Progress" (page 18). Read aloud each of the first three Scripture passages, one at a time, and ask the students to reflect in silence after each. Then ask them to the question about the three passages, perhaps sharing their thoughts in groups of two or three.

Introduce the next passage from Jeremiah with these words:

> *God calls each of us to be a "prophet," just as God called Jeremiah. In the first chapter of Jeremiah, we read how Jeremiah protested against this calling, claiming that he was too young to be a prophet and did not know how to speak. He was only a teenager. Well, God did not let Jeremiah get away with that excuse. And God doesn't let us get away with it either. Listen and reflect on these words carefully.*

Invite the students to write reflections to the questions following the Jeremiah passage. If time permits, invite students to share their reflections in small groups or as a whole class.

What Nelson Mandela says about us

Read aloud the words of Nelson Mandela, perhaps having students read them aloud as a whole group a second time for emphasis. (These words, generally attributed to Mandela, were actually quoted by him from Marianne Williamson's book *A Return to Love*.) Ask students to answer the first question and then share their answers in small groups.

Step 4—What students say about themselves

Introduction

Distribute the student handout "This Is Me, A Gifted Child of God, A 'Star'" (page 19), and read the instructions. Give additional examples of each of the three categories—skills, qualities, and experiences—to open students' imaginations about the range of gifts with which God has blessed them. Remind them to write only inside the star, because at a later time other students will be invited to write on the outside of each star. Be sure they put their names at the top or bottom.

Reflection and discussion

Ask students to fill in their star with words or short phrases, writing as many specifics as they can for each of the three categories. You might conclude this exercise by encouraging students to go outside tonight and look up at the stars in the sky. Ask them to think about those huge yet inanimate stars God created long ago and about themselves as "stars" being created by God in the present. Invite them to share their thoughts with God prayerfully in that setting.

   Note: As an option, you might give each student a large piece of newsprint and ask them to draw a much larger star. This will make it easier for students to post their stars and have other students write affirmations on the outside of each star.

Step 5—What others have to say about them

Affirmations from family

Invite the students to share their stars with some or all of their family members and invite these family members to write on the outside of their stars some of the positive things they see in the student.

Affirmations from classmates

Young people often put down one another and find it difficult to say positive things about one another. Have students post their stars around the classroom at a height where they can easily write on them. Invite them to visit these stars, read them, and write on the outside of each classmate's star at least one thing (a skill or quality) they see in that person.

Reflection and sharing

Ask the students to share their feelings and thoughts about doing these stars, both for themselves and others.

Step 6—Sharing the experience with God

Letter to God

As a way of reflecting on their dignity as children of God and as God's own work of art in progress, as a way of thanking God for the gifts they have been given, and as a way of pledging to God to use these gifts for others, invite students to write a letter to God, perhaps on the back of their "This Is Me" handout. Encourage them to choose a quiet, prayerful environment. You might give students the option of sharing their letters with you, a family member, and/or a classmate.

Concluding prayer and/or song

As a way of concluding this activity, use a popular song or poem expressing our dignity as God's works of art in progress. For example, Whitney Houston's "Greatest Love of All" touched people of all ages two decades ago. Ask students to hold their "star" handout as they pray, sing, or listen. Invite spontaneous prayers of thanksgiving. If you want to use Scripture as well, consider Mary's Magnificat (Luke 1:46–55). This is her hymn of praise and thanksgiving for what God had blessed her with and how she truly "magnified" God. Introduce it with a note that we all "magnify" God by the way we use the gifts that God has given us.

You Are God's Work of Art in Progress

What God says about us in Scripture

You have made [humans] little less than the angels and crowned [them] with glory and honor. —Psalm 8:5–6

Like clay in the hand of the potter, so are you in my hand. . . . —Jeremiah 18:6

I have called you friends. . . . It was not you who chose me, but I who chose you and appointed you to go and bear fruit that will remain. . . . —John 15:15–16

➤ *What do these passages say to you about your worth in the eyes of God?*

The word of the Lord came to me thus: Before I formed you in the womb I knew you, before you were born I dedicated you, a prophet to the nations I appointed you. "Ah, Lord God!" I said, "I know not how to speak; I am too young." But the Lord answered me, "Say not, 'I am too young.' To whomever I send you, you shall go; whatever I command you, you shall speak. Have no fear before them, because I am with you to deliver you, says the Lord." Then the Lord extended his hand and touched my mouth, saying, "See, I place my words in your mouth! . . ." —Jeremiah 1:4–9

➤ *When you think about God calling you to be a prophet, not to a whole nation as Jeremiah was, but at least to a few people, how do you feel?*

➤ *How has God used you in the past to speak out for others? How do you think God might want to use you as a prophet right now? Later in life?*

What Nelson Mandela says about us

When he was inaugurated as President of South Africa after spending twenty-seven years in a prison because of his efforts to change the apartheid government, Nelson Mandela challenged his people with these words:

Our deepest fear is not that we are inadequate. Our deepest fear is that we are powerful beyond measure. It is our light, not our darkness, that most frightens us. We ask ourselves, "Who am I to be brilliant, gorgeous, talented and fabulous?" Actually, who are you not to be? You are a child of God. Your playing small doesn't serve the world. There is nothing enlightened about shrinking so that other people won't feel insecure around you. . . . We are born to make manifest the glory of God that is within us. It's not just in some of us; it's in everyone. . . .

➤ *What words or phrases strike you the most? Underline them. What feelings do they generate inside you?*

➤ *Have you ever hid your talents and "played small"? When and why?*

➤ *In what ways do you already manifest the glory of God?*

THIS IS ME, A GIFTED CHILD OF GOD, A "STAR"

➤ **Inside the star, write**

⭐ all the skills and abilities (e.g., writing, artistic expression, emotional or physical strengths) that you have in some degree;

⭐ all your personal inner qualities (e.g., kindness, compassion, ability to observe or listen deeply, patience, forgiveness);

⭐ some of the special experiences (e.g., special people in your life, special places you've been, special jobs or volunteer opportunities you've had, camps you've participated in) that God has provided through others that have helped to shape who you are.

Chapter 1, Activity 2

Service and Random Acts of Kindness

Step 1—Introduction

Since Catholic social teaching emphasizes the need to put faith into action, words into deeds, this activity is designed to reinforce the gospel message of sacrificial service of others, that Jesus came not be served but to serve. In addition to Jesus, three other models of service are lifted up for inspiration and practical suggestions for action—Mother Teresa, Martin Luther King, Jr., and twelve-year-old Trevor, the model of service in the movie *Pay It Forward*. Students are challenged to reflect on their own lives and hopes for the future and to decide now to make service of others more integral to their lives.

This activity builds on the segments in the student text on "What Jesus Reveals About Being Human" (pages 18–19) and the profile of Mother Teresa, pages 24–25.

Depending on the length of your class periods, this activity might best be done in two sessions, with students encouraged to do the "extended reflection" at the end of step 4 as homework.

Step 2—Jesus as our model of service

Reflection

Ask students to read (or summarize yourself) "What Jesus Reveals About Being Human," pages 18–19, and underline phrases or sentences that stand out for them. Invite them to share or name something from the reading that touched them. If time permits, share one of the phrases that touched you and why.

Further scriptural reflection

Read both John 15:12 and Matthew 25:31–46 to the group. Ask students what these words of Jesus mean to them.

Step 3—Mother Teresa as a model of service

Reflection and sharing

Have the students read (or summarize for them) the profile of Mother Teresa in their text, pages 24–25. Ask students to share a prominent impression they have of Mother Teresa.

Discussion

Reread aloud the last two sentences and ask students the following questions:

- Who are some of the "no matter how small" people Mother Teresa is referring to?

- What does she mean by "every person is Jesus-in-disguise"?

- How can you live more like Mother Teresa?

Step 4—Dr. King as a model of service

Discussion

Distribute the handout "Dr. King's Own Eulogy and Yours" (page 24) and choose several students to read it aloud, perhaps a different person for each sentence. Invite student observations or questions on Dr. King's eulogy.

Reflection and sharing

Have the students answer the first two questions under "Your own eulogy" and invite them to share their answers in groups of two or three. If time permits, invite some sharing with the whole class.

Extended reflection

As an optional homework activity, invite students to write the first paragraph of their own eulogy on the back of the handout. These could be used as a kind of "pre-test" at the beginning of this course, with the invitation to rewrite their eulogy at the end of the course to see how they have changed. For more visually or artistically oriented students, you might encourage them to create a collage with captions or illustrate a poem to serve as as their eulogies.

Step 5—Random acts of kindness

View or summarize Pay It Forward

The movie *Pay It Forward* (2000) is available in popular release at the video store. In response to his seventh grade social studies assignment to create something that will help change the world, Trevor designs a "pay it forward" scheme of doing difficult random acts of kindness for three people. In return, they don't pay him back; instead they pay it forward by doing acts of kindness to three others, and so on. Trevor succeeds in doing two, but is afraid to do the third one—defending a classmate against bigger students who have been harassing him. As the "pay it forward" movement spreads, Trevor finds the courage to do his third act of kindness and pays for it with his life. It's a touching example of Jesus' sacrificial love on the cross.

Note: If it isn't feasible to have students view the whole video, either in class or on their own, summarize the story, without describing the dramatic ending, and show only the final twelve minutes.

Discussion

Ask students to share their impressions of the video. If they don't surface the question, be sure to discuss whether they think Trevor's act was worth its cost.

Reflection and brainstorm

Ask students to answer in writing questions 3 and 4 on their handout. Invite students to share their answers with the whole class and list the various acts of kindness that are identified.

Decision

Based on what they wrote and heard about various acts of kindness, invite each student to answer question 5.

Step 6—Prayer service

Use the handout "Prayer Service on Service" (page 25) to conclude this activity. Choose one or more students as readers.

DR. KING'S OWN EULOGY AND YOURS

A Drum Major for Justice

. . . I'd like somebody to mention that day that Martin Luther King, Jr., tried to give his life serving others.

I'd like for somebody to say that day that Martin Luther King, Jr., tried to love somebody.

I want you to say that I tried to be right on the war question.

I want you to be able to say that day that I did try in my life to clothe those who were naked.

I want you to say on that day that I did try in my life to visit those who were in prison.

And I want you to say that I tried to love and serve humanity. . . .

And that is all I want to say. If I can help somebody as I pass along; if I can cheer somebody with a song; if I can show somebody he's traveling wrong; then my living will not be in vain. . . .

—Martin Luther King, Jr.

(From "Then My Living Will Not Be in Vain," Ebenezer Baptist Church, February 1968; in A Testament of Hope: The Essential Writings and Speeches of Martin Luther King, Jr., *p. 267.)*

Your own eulogy and acts of kindness

1. *Make a list of what you will need to do so that you will be able to say that "my living will not be in vain."*

2. *Dr. King entitled his own eulogy "A Drum Major for Justice." What would you like the title of your eulogy to be?*

3. *What are some of the random acts of kindness that you occasionally do?*

4. *What else are you already doing at home, at school, in the community, at church to be of service to others?*

5. *If you "tried to give [your] life serving others," as Dr. King did, what more could you do right now to put that into practice? Choose one act of kindness and commit to doing it regularly for the next month.*

PRAYER SERVICE ON SERVICE

READER: *As Mother Teresa has told us, "Do something beautiful for God. Every person, no matter how small, is a person of great dignity. Every person is Jesus-in-disguise."*

RESPONSE: *Mother Teresa, disciple of Jesus, help us to do this—to do something beautiful for God by reaching out to someone in need. Jesus, help us to see you in each person we encounter today and every day, especially those who might especially need our smile, a kind word, or a helping hand.*

READER: *As Dr. King has told us, ". . . I'd like somebody to mention that day that Martin Luther King, Jr., tried to give his life serving others."*

RESPONSE: *Dr. King, disciple of Jesus, help us to give our lives serving others, day by day, starting with today. Jesus, servant of all, help us follow you by serving others.*

READER: *"I want you to be able to say that day that I did try in my life to clothe those who were naked . . . that I did try in my life to visit those who were in prison."*

RESPONSE: *Help us, Dr. King, to share our clothes and time with those in need and pray for all who are imprisoned.*

READER: *As Jesus has told us, "Whatever you did for one of these least brothers or sisters of mine, you did for me."*

RESPONSE: *Jesus, help us seek out the least of your people, not avoid or avert our eyes from them. Help us to serve them, for in serving them, we are serving you.*

READER: *Jesus, in those important last words you gave your disciples before your agony and death, you told us that this is your commandment: "Love one another as I love you. No one has greater love than this, to lay down one's life for one's friends" (John 15:12–13).*

RESPONSE: *Jesus, help us to love as you loved. Help us to lay down our lives in some way each day to help someone else who needs our attention, our time, and our love.*

READER: *And as Dr. King told us in conclusion, "And that is all I want to say. If I can help somebody as I pass along; if I can cheer somebody with a song; if I can show somebody he's traveling wrong; then my living will not be in vain. . . ."*

RESPONSE: *Jesus, help us follow your example as we pass along our life's journey, cheering those who need to be cheered, challenging someone who needs to be challenged, helping those you send our way. For we believe that in following you in service to others, our living will not be in vain.*

Chapter 2

Justice and Virtues

(See pages 29–51 of *Catholic Social Teaching*)

Justice itself is a virtue which enables us to give to God and others their rights. This chapter focuses on types of justice as well as the theological virtues—faith, hope, and charity—which have their origin in God.

Chapter 2, Activity 1

Charity and Justice: The Two Feet of Christian Service

Step 1—Introduction

This activity is designed to build on the comparison between charity and justice (see page 34 of the Student Text) and apply it to the segment on César Chávez (see page 45 of the Student Text). It challenges students to reflect on their own life and find ways of integrating both charity and justice into their responses to injustice.

Step 2—"Babies in the River"—An Allegory

Reflection and sharing

Distribute the handout "The Works of Justice as Well as the Works of Charity" (page 30) and read the allegory of the "Babies in the River." Ask students to choose their response and write their reason for doing so. Invite them to share their responses in groups of two or three.

Discussion

Ask the students what the point of the allegory is and then brainstorm some of what the person(s) "going upstream" might find and what could be done about those sources of this tragedy. Ask the students for comparable situations actually occurring in their community, nation, and world. For example, the flood of immigrants from Mexico to the United States. Discuss what some of the sources of this kind of "flood" might be (e.g., poverty, persecution, a sense of hopelessness).

Step 3—The works of charity and the works of justice

Background

Both direct service (the works of charity or mercy) and social change (the works of justice) are part of the Christian response to the needs and injustices in our society. Christians of all ages are generally more comfortable and familiar with the works of charity. The "corporal works of mercy" are cataloged in Catholic social teaching as well as Scripture (see Matthew 25:31–46). We need to help students identify a range of possible works of justice and find the opportunities, compassion, and courage to do them.

Discussion

Using the categories of actions listed in the "Justice . . . Social Change" column of the chart on page 34 of the Student Text, take the first work of charity—helping at a soup kitchen—and brainstorm various ways of addressing the causes of hunger. To involve all students in this creative thinking, divide the class into small groups for brainstorming the corresponding works of justice for each of the other works of charity, one work of charity for each small group. Invite the small groups to report on their list of works of justice.

Decisions

Invite the students to identify any works of justice that they have done in the past and/or are doing in the present. Then invite them to make a decision about whether there is some work of justice they would be willing to begin doing or continue doing at this time.

Step 4—Case study: César Chávez and the United Farm Workers

Reading

Assign the description of César Chávez on page 45 of the Student Text. Answer any clarification questions the students might have.

A family conflict

Present the following debate between a young activist and his father.

In the late 1960s when César Chávez was organizing California farm workers into the United Farm Workers Union, the Catholic bishops of California urged Christian Brothers Wines to recognize the Union. This created a problem for one young activist who supported the UFW and his father who worked for Christian Brothers. The father was adamant about his position—the workers don't need a union because the growers that Christian Brothers worked with took good care of their workers. He pointed out to his son that the growers often paid for the health care needs of their workers and were very generous with Christmas gifts, and that he had personally donated to help these workers. The growers knew what their workers needed and were providing it. Besides, the union leaders weren't very educated and some of them were just out for themselves. The son acknowledged his father's points, but argued that the workers had the right to bargain for wages and working conditions that would enable them to meet their own needs without depending on the growers' generosity.

Discussion

Raise the following questions with students.

- Which is the main issue of the debate between father and son?

- Which person do you agree with more and why?

- Based on what you know about Catholic social teaching from your text, which position do you think is more basic to Catholic social teaching and why?

THE WORKS OF JUSTICE AS WELL AS THE WORKS OF CHARITY

1. "Babies in the River"—An Allegory

One day, a group of picnickers along a river noticed several babies floating down the river. They jumped in to rescue them and noticed even more babies floating by. They called to others to help and before long there was a string of people involved in the rescue operation. As more and more babies appeared in the river, people began organizing temporary shelter along the bank. Medical people were called in. Milk and other foods were gathered. Eventually, a team of social workers began to arrange foster care for those babies strong enough not to be hospitalized. Finally, one person started walking upstream along the shore. As babies continued to float down the river, others shouted at the person to stay and help. The person turned and answered: "I'm going upstream to try to stop whoever or whatever is throwing the babies into the river."

➤ *If you were picnicking nearby and saw what was happening, what would have been your response and why?*

☐ Picnic somewhere else

☐ Jump into the river and help babies out

☐ Go for other help (what kind?)

☐ Join the person going upstream

2. "Two Feet of Christian Service"

For each of the works of charity or direct service identified in the "Foot of Charity," identify at least one work of justice that addresses the need in the first place.

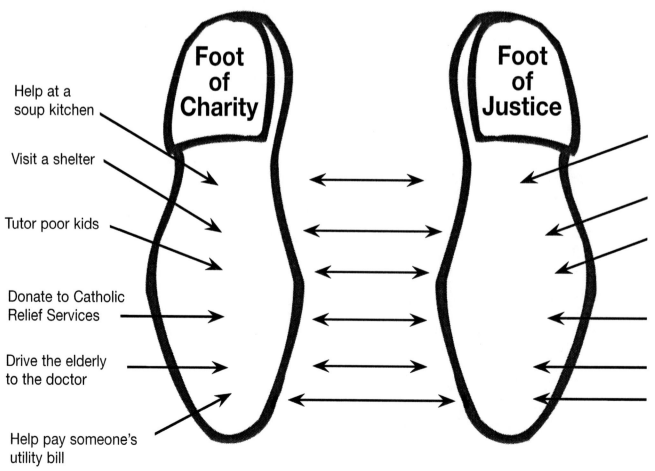

Help at a
soup kitchen

Visit a shelter

Tutor poor kids

Donate to Catholic
Relief Services

Drive the elderly
to the doctor

Help pay someone's
utility bill

Foot
of
Charity

Foot
of
Justice

Chapter 2, Activity 2

Social Justice as the Redistribution of Power

Step 1—Introduction

This activity is designed to highlight key principles of social justice—the right of *participation*, the right *to be heard*. It challenges students to move beyond their usual understanding of justice as primarily a redistribution of the goods of creation. This principle of participation is enhanced by the diagram on the student handout, "From Vertical Relationships to Horizontal Relationships," on page 34, by an examination of the major social relationships, and by a key passage from a pastoral letter of the Appalachian Bishops. Finally, the students are challenged to apply these principles to their own lives, especially in a school setting.

Step 2—Contrast distributive justice and social justice

Description

On pages 32–34 of the Student Text, social justice is contrasted with distributive justice. While distributive justice is concerned about a just distribution of the goods of creation, the focus of social justice is everyone's "right to be heard"—the right to participate in the decisions that affect one's life. In other words, distributive justice requires a redistribution of goods, while social justice requires a redistribution of power.

A redistribution of goods without a redistribution of power is called "paternalism." Thus, *how* the goods of creation are provided is as important as *that* they are provided. A redistribution of goods often happens only because the poor begin to organize themselves, discover their power, and demand a more just distribution of these goods.

Visual contrast

Another word for injustice is domination, while another word for social justice is empower-ment. Injustice/domination is visualized as a vertical relationship between those on top, the dominators, and those on the bottom, the dominated. Justice/empowerment is visualized as a horizontal relationship between co-equal partners. The challenge, then, for social justice is to turn every vertical relationship into a more horizontal relationship.

Discussion

To help the students better understand this critical difference between vertical and horizontal relationships and the task of social justice, ask them to locate on the diagram the various pairs presented in the student handout "From Vertical Relationships to Horizontal Relationships" (page 34) and place each pair either on the vertical or horizontal bar depending on where they think the pair belongs.

Step 3—"Those who make the rules get the goods"

Whole group discussion

Poll the class on how many think the statement "Those who make the rules get the goods" is generally true. Then choose one of the sets of pairs from the top of the handout, perhaps "workers and management," and discuss who makes the rules and who gets most of the goods.

Small groups and conclusions

Assign each of the remaining sets of relationships to a small group for closer consideration. Ask each group to report its findings. Ask students what general conclusions they can draw from this exploration.

Step 4—How to empower and give voice to those on the bottom

Description

Read aloud the passage from the Catholic Bishops of Appalachia and discuss briefly the first two questions that follow the passage.

Empowerment in their own lives

To engage students in this key question, start with the same set of relationships you used in step 3. Save "parents and children" and "students and teachers" for step 5. Consider as many of the others as time permits.

Step 5—Social justice for youth

Discussion of social justice at school

Ask students for their initial thoughts on how they could exercise their "voice" in their relationships with teachers and administration. What are the various ways they can participate in decision-making in the classroom and school? Distribute the student handout "Principles for Class Meetings" (page 35) and discuss how these meetings could be implemented with this group. Brainstorm additional principles or suggestions for conducting class meetings.

Decision

Decide with your students whether to try class meetings as part of this course on Catholic social teaching, which principles to start with, and how to implement them.

FROM VERTICAL RELATIONSHIPS TO HORIZONTAL RELATIONSHIPS

1. Injustice/domination vs. Social justice/empowerment

➤ *On the diagram opposite, ranging from totally vertical to totally horizontal, place the following pairs of relationships:*

INJUSTICE

SOCIAL JUSTICE | EMPOWERMENT

DOMINATION

- Women and men
- Workers and management
- The poor and the wealthy
- Parents and children
- Students and teachers
- Clergy and laity
- Citizens and politicians
- The human species and all other species
- Developed nations and developing nations
- People of color and Caucasians

➤ Which of these relationships are as they should be? Why?
➤ Which ones need to be changed? Why?

2. "Those who make the rules get the goods"

➤ *Do you believe this is true? For each set of pairs above, who makes the rules that govern their relationship? In each case, do those who make the rules get most or all of the goods or the benefits?*

3. Empowerment and voice

Consider these words from the Catholic Bishops of Appalachia in This Land Is Home to Me, *as they describe the process they went through in writing this landmark pastoral letter.*

> *Throughout this whole process of listening to the people, the goal which underlies our concern is fundamental in the justice struggle, namely, citizen control or community control. The people themselves must shape their own destiny. Despite the theme of powerlessness, we know that Appalachia is already rich here in the cooperative power of its own people.*

➤ *How did these bishops empower their people?*

➤ *What does "citizen control or community control" mean?*

➤ *In each set of relationships above, how can both voices in the relationship be heard?*

PRINCIPLES FOR CLASS MEETINGS

Regularly scheduled

➤ After an initial trial run, schedule class meetings regularly so that there is some predictability.

Make the agenda available to everyone

➤ Have a box available in which to put agenda items. Make sure everyone knows that class meetings are to deal with overall class matters, not personal issues between students or between students and teacher. A committee consisting of the teacher and two students (to be rotated) would select the appropriate items and prioritize them. If they didn't understand a particular item put in the box, check with that person before the meeting to clarify the item and decide whether it should be on the agenda.

Clear rules and everyone has a chance to speak

➤ Establish a set of rules that everyone agrees to; e.g., no one speaks a second time on an item until everyone has a chance to speak, raise your hand if you want to speak, no name calling, etc.

Brainstorm alternatives before deciding

➤ Don't always settle on the first solution proposed. Don't criticize brainstormed possibilities right away. Identify a number of possible solutions and then evaluate each one.

Decide by consensus

➤ Voting usually means some win and some lose. If at all possible, choose a solution that everyone is at least willing to try for a short time, even if they aren't sure it will work. If you can't reach a consensus, carry the item over to the next meeting.

Quality vs. quantity

➤ Don't try to finish all the items on the agenda for a particular meeting if some items are taking more time than anticipated. Carry the less urgent items over to the next meeting, if necessary.

Rotate leadership

➤ This helps to develop everyone's leadership skills and creates a greater sense of equality.

Clear and written decisions

➤ Be sure that the decisions are clear, tasks are assigned, consequences are identified when necessary, and that a check-in time is identified (i.e., a time to evaluate how well a particular solution is working).

Other suggestions?

Chapter 2, Activity 3

God's Justice in Scripture

Step 1—Introduction

This activity supplements the Scripture passages on pages 35–38 of the Student Text and provides a process for reflecting on these passages. The concluding step of creating a visual representation of God's justice engages the imagination and utilizes other gifts that students have, helping to balance the reflect-and-discuss approach in the first five steps.

This activity and the student handout are adapted from more comprehensive treatments of Amos and the other Hebrew prophets in *Teaching the Prophets; Living as Prophets* by James McGinnis (Institute for Peace and Justice, 2004) and on the justice of Jesus in *If Only Today You Knew . . . The Things That Make for Peace*, by James McGinnis (Institute for Peace and Justice, 2003).

Step 2—God's providing for the Hebrew people

Discussing the Exodus passage

Distribute the handout "God's Justice in Scripture" (page 41). From the first section of the handout, read aloud the passage from Exodus 16:13–32 and explain any unfamiliar terms. Ask the students how many of them would have been tempted to gather more than they needed (verse 17), would have kept something for the next day (verse 20), or tried to gather some on the seventh day (verse 27), and why. Then ask students what they think God was telling the Hebrew people about how to live justly.

Discussing the Leviticus passage

Read aloud Leviticus 25:1–7 and ask the students what they think God was telling the Hebrew people about how to live justly in relationship to the land. Repeat this for verses 8–43, asking students what they think God was telling the Hebrew people about how to live justly in relationship to one another.

Application question

Conclude this step by asking students how we can apply these actions and principles to our own lives and to our economic system to make them more just.

Step 3—God's vision and challenge through the prophet Amos

Background on Amos

Read aloud the three-line description of Amos on the student handout. If you want to provide additional background, you might add that Amos was a shepherd and a dresser of fig trees, a "farm worker" in today's terms. He lived in Tekoa, a small town twelve miles south of Jerusalem, part of the southern kingdom of Judah. Around 750 BC, God came to him while he was "following the flock" and made him a prophet. He was poor, tough, crude at times, had no formal education, and was regarded as an "outside agitator" by Israel's leaders. His message was a ringing indictment of the luxuriousness of the wealthy and the injustice of a growing merchant class that exploited the poor and controlled their lands, producing export crops like wine and oil while the poor went hungry. The legal system supported this exploitation, taking bribes and not dispensing justice "at the gate."

Discussing the passages

With each passage from Amos, read the passage twice and ask students what they think Amos means, what specific practices he is identifying.

Applying the passages

Ask students to reflect in silence briefly on the application questions following the passages, one question at a time. Invite them to share their reflections with the whole group. If after the first set of passages and questions you think the process would be more engaging for all students by having them share their reflections in groups of two or three, do so. Return to the whole group format if you sense that the small groups aren't working well.

Step 4—The justice of Jesus goes beyond fairness

Discussing the passages

Assign the four passages on the handout to four different small groups. Ask each group to read the full passage and then discuss the question, "How does the justice of Jesus go beyond fairness in this passage?" Ask each group to share with the whole group what they learned about the "justice of Jesus" in their discussion.

Applying the passages

Ask each student to answer in writing the question, "What is Jesus asking of us in these passages?" Invite them to share their answers in their small groups or in pairs. If time permits, invite them to share their reflections with the whole class.

Step 5—The early Christian community's sense of distributive justice

Discussing the passages

Read aloud to the whole class the two passages from Acts on the student handout and ask students why or why not this principle of living according to need seems just to them and and whether or not they would like to live that way. Read aloud 2 Corinthians 8:13–15 and discuss whether this seems just.

Applying the passages

Ask students how they could apply this sense of distributive justice to their own lives and to our economic system to make it more just.

Step 6—Visualizing God's justice

Creating a visual

As a way of summarizing this activity and touching into students' imaginations, invite them to create some kind of visual representation of God's justice, as they understand it. It could be a drawing, a collage of pictures, a symbol or artifact, or a combination of any of these.

Sharing their creations

Provide an opportunity for students to present and explain their visual representations.

GOD'S JUSTICE IN SCRIPTURE

1. God's providing for the Hebrew people

Exodus 16:13–32—Manna in the desert. During the forty years of wandering in the desert, God fed the people one "omer" of manna per day. This was sufficient and no one received more than they needed and no one received less than they needed.

Leviticus 25—Sabbatical and jubilee years. As a way of insuring the well-being of everyone, every seventh year ("sabbatical year") and every fiftieth year ("jubilee year") those who went into debt, lost their land, or were sold into slavery were restored to their rightful dignity as a free child of God.

➤ *What was God telling the Hebrew people about how to live justly in each passage?*

➤ *How could we apply these actions and principles to our own lives and to our economic system to make them more just?*

2. God's vision and challenge through Amos

This eighth-century BC Hebrew prophet challenged the luxurious lifestyles and exploitative economic practices of the new merchant class as well as the upper class and proclaimed that worship without justice is empty.

"Hear this word, women of the mountain of Samaria, you cows of Bashan, you who oppress the weak and abuse the needy; who say to your lords, 'Bring drink for us!' . . ." (4:1–3).

➤ *Who are the "cows of Bashan" of our own time and what is being said to them? Do any of these indictments apply to us as well? For what?*

"Because you have trampled upon the weak and exacted from them levies of grain, though you have built houses of hewn stone, you shall not live in them! Though you have planted choice vineyards, you shall not drink their wine! Yes, I know how many are your crimes, how grievous your sins: oppressing the just, accepting bribes, repelling the needy at the gate" (5:11–12).

➤ *Is our own economic and/or legal system being called to change in this passage? Do any of these indictments apply to us as well? For what?*

"I hate, I spurn your feasts; I take no pleasure in your solemnities . . . But let justice surge like water, and goodness like an unfailing stream" (5:21–24).

➤ *What is true worship of God? Is any of the worship in our country "false"? Do we personally worship the way God wants? Is there anything we can or should do differently, as a nation? As individuals?*

3. The justice of Jesus goes beyond fairness

Luke 15:11–32—"the prodigal son"

Matthew 20:1–16—paying a full day's wage to all workers, even those working only the last hour.

Matthew 18:21–22—"Lord, if my brother sins against me, how often must I forgive him?" . . . Seventy-seven times."

Matthew 5:38–48—"You have heard that it was said: 'An eye for an eye and a tooth for a tooth.' . . . But I say to you, when someone strikes you on your right cheek, turn the other one to him as well. . . ."

➤ *How does the justice of Jesus go beyond fairness?*

➤ *What is Jesus asking of us in these passages?*

4. The early Christian community's sense of distributive justice

Sharing according to need—Acts 2:42–47 and 4:32–35.

Sharing our surplus with those in need—2 Corinthians 8:13–15. Paul asks the people of Corinth to be generous in making donations to the impovershed Church in Jerusalem, based on the principle of equality. ". . . As a matter of equality your surplus at the present time should supply their needs, so that their surplus may also supply your needs, that there may be equality. As it is written: 'Whoever had much did not have more, and whoever had little did not have less.'"

➤ *How could we apply this sense of distributive justice to our own lives and to our economic system to make it more just?*

5. Images of God's justice

➤ *From these passages across four different biblical times, how would you describe God's understanding of justice in images? Draw a picture or symbol(s) of God's justice or put together a collage of pictures, symbols, and/or artifacts on a separate page that express your understanding of God's justice.*

Chapter 2, Activity 4

"What Does the Lord Require of You?"

Step 1—Introduction

This activity is designed to highlight the biblical segments of the chapter, to amplify the understanding of biblical justice as right relationships, and then to use Micah 6:8 as a way to summarize the message, practically and prayerfully. In order to help students understand what God is asking of them through Micah 6:8, several translations of each phrase are listed. The translation used for their reflection is taken from the lyrics of a inspiring song by Christian musicians Jim and Jean Strathdee, entitled "What Does the Lord Require?" (from *Jubilee* and included here with their permission). The other translations, in order, are from the *New American Bible*, the *Jerusalem Bible*, and the *Children's Bible*.

Note: If you want to link this activity with the works of justice identified in the other activities in this chapter, you could add another action option: The Micah Challenge, a global campaign to mobilize Christians against poverty (see www.micahchallenge.org).

Step 2—Biblical justice as right relationships

Expanding the text

Biblical justice is variously described in the Student Text as "fidelity to what relationships require" (page 35) and "fidelity to God, neighbor and to God's created goods" (page 36).

- **Right relationship with God.** We are faithful to God when we are faithful to God's covenant and "obey God and lead upright, just lives." "Upright and just lives" is more specifically identified in the Old Testament as compassion for the orphans, widows, and aliens (foreigners).

- **Right relationship with neighbor** includes everyone, especially foreigners, the weak, and the poor. Following the example of Jesus, it means doing justice to the point of sacrificial love.

- **Right relationship with God's created goods** means right relationship with the earth. The Student Text quotes Saint Ambrose (page 38) to show that this means using only what we need and sharing what we don't need with those who do.

Highlighting the connections

Justice is the key. A right relationship with our neighbor and with creation is integral to a right relationship with God.

- **God and neighbor.** How clearly love of God is identified with love of neighbor, especially the poor, is revealed in Jeremiah 22:16, where Jeremiah compares the new king with his father, saying that "Because he dispensed justice to the weak and the poor, it went well with him. Is this not true knowledge of me? says the Lord." Biblical "knowledge" means "intimate relationship." An intimate relationship with God requires promoting justice for the weak and poor. Chapter 7 focuses on this as the basis of God's "preferential option for the poor."

- **God and the earth.** The connection between love of God and care for the goods of God's creation is boldly stated in Psalm 24:1—"The earth is the Lord's and all that it holds." We are stewards of God's creation. You want to love God? Then love God's creation! In Micah 6:8, the connection is more subtle. The words "humbly" and "human" both come from the same root—"humus"—which means earth. Walking humbly with our Creator means embracing our creature and reverencing the dignity of all other forms of life that God has created, not exploiting creation for our own benefit.

Step 3—Making Micah meaningful

Reading the passage

Distribute the student handout "Making Micah Meaningful" (page 47) and introduce the passage (Micah 6:8) as a key summary statement about justice, understood as right relationships with God, neighbor, and the earth; and the clearest call from God to make justice a "constitutive" dimension of our lives. Read together the translation of the passage as it is in the Student Text, on page 36.

Discussion

Read the questions on the handout under "What does the Lord require of you?" and brainstorm the various ways to discern the specifics of God's call. In case their answers don't include the following, you should add them to the list: reading the Scriptures, asking for the Holy Spirit's guidance, listening silently to God in prayer, studying Church teaching, discussing all this honestly and courageously with other people of faith, and reflecting on the actions you take to put this into practice.

Introduction of the four sections of the handout

These represent the four dimensions of biblical justice, the four aspects of right relationships. Right relationship with our neighbor involves both justice and love. You might also call the students' attention to the various translations of each dimension.

- **"To seek justice"** parallels the virtue of justice and the works of justice. It represents the *prophetic* dimension of ministry.

- **"And love kindness"** parallels the virtue of charity and the works of charity or mercy. It represents the *pastoral* dimension of ministry.

- **"And walk humbly with your God"** contains both our right relationship with God and with God's creation. They represent what might be called the *prayerful* and *careful* dimensions of ministry.

Small group discussion

Assign each of these four dimensions of justice and ministry to four different small groups, perhaps several small groups per dimension, depending on the size of your class. Invite students to identify both specific situations where their dimension is needed and specific ways to apply it in those situations.

Personal decision

Invite students to make a decision about one specific way they will each put their reflection into action. Allow time for individuals to share their decisions in their small groups.

Step 4—Praying Micah 6:8

Use the student handout "Praying Micah 6:8" (page 48) as the way to prayerfully conclude this activity. If you want to involve the students more fully in this step, invite each discussion group or a representative of each group to formulate a second "Group" petition for each of the four segments in the space provided in the final litany, based on the specific ways they identified in their discussions for putting their particular segment of Micah's message into practice.

MAKING MICAH MEANINGFUL

"What does the Lord require of you?"

Other translations boldly state that "You have already been told what is right and what Yahweh wants of you: Only this. . . ." Yes, you already know God's general requirements, but how do you figure out what God requires of you in the specific situations of your life? How do you discern what God wants you to do in seeking justice, or loving tenderly, or walking humbly with God on this earth?

"To seek justice"—Prophetic ministry
(or "do what is right," "do the right," "act justly," "see that justice is done")

➤ *Identify some specific situations in your life where you need to seek justice and some specific ways to seek justice in those situations.*

"And love kindness"—Pastoral ministry
(or "love loyalty," "love goodness," "love tenderly," "let mercy be your first concern")

➤ *Identify some specific situations in your life where you especially need to love tenderly and then some specific ways to love kindly or tenderly in those situations.*

"And walk humbly with your God"—Prayerful ministry
(or "And humbly obey your God")

➤ *Identify some reasons why a prayerful relationship with God is so important for justice ministry and then some specific ways to be more prayerful with God.*

"And walk humbly with the goods of your God's creation"—Careful ministry

➤ *Identify some specific situations in your life where you especially need to walk humbly or carefully with the goods of God's creation and some specific ways of doing this.*

PRAYING MICAH 6:8

Group: Creator God, you have a dream for your creation. And you have created us for a purpose, to assist you in realizing your dream. So what is it that you require of us?

Micah: "You have already been told what is right and what Yahweh wants of you."

Group: Revealing God, help us read your word more faithfully and listen more carefully to your Spirit speaking to our spirits.

Micah: If you truly want to know what God wants of you, it is this and only this: to seek justice . . .

Group: God of justice, help us to open our eyes and hearts to the injustices all around us and see the faces of your people who are being exploited, discriminated against, cast aside. Give us the courage to speak up for your people, whether it's to political leaders, corporations, or to our own families and friends.

Micah: If you still want to know what God wants of you, it is this and only this: to love tenderly . . .

Group: God of mercy and love, you love all your children with a mother's tenderness. Send us your Spirit of love to open our hearts to those around us. Make us the instruments of your tender love. Help us to touch others with loving eyes, with consoling words, with gentle hands.

Micah: If you still want to know what God wants of you, it is this and only this: to walk humbly with God . . .

Group: Creator God, we truly are your humble creatures. Help us always to put you first—the first thought in our minds when we awaken, the first Person we turn to for help, the first consideration when we make decisions about using the talents, time, and treasure that you have given us. Help us to place ourselves prayerfully in your presence each day.

Micah: If you still want to know what God wants of you, it is this and only this: to walk humbly and carefully with the goods of God's creation.

Group: Gracious God, you have lavished your gifts on your creation and on us your children. Help us receive what you give gratefully, tend what you give carefully, share what you give generously, and never keep for ourselves what we don't truly need when other children of yours are in need.

WHAT DOES THE LORD REQUIRE?

Chapter 3

Justice and Society

(See pages 53–73 of *Catholic Social Teaching*)

The universal call for justice exists to build the *common good*. Catholic teaching stresses the importance of establishing societies where people can develop their talents and meet their needs. Given our social nature, we are called to live in solidarity—union with our brothers and sisters throughout the world—especially with the poor.

Chapter 3, Activity 1

Interdependence Demands Solidarity

Step 1—Introduction

This activity provides an experiential supplement for the segments in the Student Text on "rugged individualism" (page 54) and the principles of the common good and solidarity (page 59–63). It builds on Pope John Paul II's statement that the reality of interdependence leads to the virtue of solidarity (page 61).

Step 2—Personal interdependence

Introductory song

Any of these popular release songs would be appealing to students to open (or conclude) this activity—"You and Me" by Lifehouse, "These Words" by Natasha Bedingfield, or "Inside Your Heaven" by Carrie Underwood. Or, allow the students to offer some suggestions for songs with lyrics that speak of both freedom and interdependence.

Discussion

Distribute the handout "Interdependence Is Our Reality" (page 55) and read aloud the quotation from Pope Paul VI. Solicit any clarification questions before asking the student to reflect on the material.

Reflection and discussion

Work through the handout. Invite students to list as many individuals and groups as they can from whom they have benefited. You might use your own life as an example, uncovering some of the relationships they might not consider. Invite students to share with the whole group some of those they identified in each category. Encourage them to write down additional individuals and groups as they listen to others' lists.

Reflection

Assign to the students the writing of a prayer of thanksgiving, addressed to God and to all who have benefited them. If they need more space, ask them to use the back of the handout.

Discussion and decision

Discuss what Pope Paul VI means by his last sentence—"The reality of human solidarity, which is a benefit for us, also imposes a duty"—especially what "duty" of solidarity means and how it can be carried out. Then invite each student to choose one thing they will do to carry out this duty and then write it in the form of a pledge addressed to God, to those from whom they have benefited, and to those whom they will benefit. If they need more space, ask them to use the back of the handout.

Artistic options

Especially for students who are visual or kinesthetic learners, you might encourage students to create a collage of photos and pictures to reflect some of those from whom they have benefited so much. Their prayer of thanksgiving and/or pledge of solidarity could be in the form of a poem, a song, or perhaps a dance.

Step 3—Global interdependence is a daily reality

Discussion

Distribute the handout "Global Interdependence Is a Daily Reality" (page 56). Read aloud the excerpt from Dr. King's 1967 Christmas sermon and ask students what it says to them. Compare King's words with those of Pope John Paul II on page 61 in the Student Text.

Another example of global interdependence is something as "American" as a Hershey's Bar. While Hershey's Bars are produced in Hershey, Pennsylvania, it's the ingredients that make it a global reality. Besides the milk and corn syrup, there is sugar, perhaps from the Dominican Republic or the Philippines. The cocoa comes from Ghana or another West African country. And if your Hershey's Bar has almonds, those probably come from Brazil or perhaps from almond fields in California.

Research

Ask students to research the realities of interdependence in their daily lives. If you want to stimulate their research while in class, you might ask them to look around the room and identify what they see that probably comes in some way from other countries.

Step 4—Prayer service of thanksgiving and solidarity

Ask students to go back to their student handout "Interdependence Is Our Reality" and focus on the last two items—their prayer of thanksgiving and their pledge of solidarity.

Invite students who are willing to slowly read their prayer of thanksgiving, followed by their pledge of solidarity. You might begin this prayer service with the following words or similar words of your own.

> *Gracious God, you have invested much in each of us, through so many who came before us and so many of our contemporaries. We thank you for your generosity and for your trust that we will use your gifts on behalf of others, just as others have used their gifts to benefit us. We make our pledges of solidarity today, trusting that your Spirit of courage and compassion will empower us and that your Spirit of mercy will reach out to us when we fall short of your hopes for us.*

INTERDEPENDENCE IS OUR REALITY

"No one is an island"

Consider this passage from Pope Paul VI:

"*. . . Each person is a member of society. Each is part of the whole of humankind. It is not just certain individuals, but all persons who are called to this fullness of development. Civilizations are born, develop and die. But humanity is advancing along the path of history like the waves of a rising tide encroaching gradually on the shore. We have inherited from past generations and have benefited from the work of our contemporaries; for this reason we have obligations toward all, and we cannot refuse to interest ourselves in those who will come after us to enlarge the human family. The reality of human solidarity, which is a benefit for us, also imposes a duty*" (Pope Paul VI, On the Development of Peoples, 1967, #17).

➤ *Make a list of family ancestors and identify at least one thing (e.g., a talent, an interest, a possession, inheritance, etc.) you have received in some way from each of them.*

➤ *List all the contemporaries (family members, teachers, counselors, coaches, pastors, youth leaders, etc.) from whose work you have benefited and what they have given you.*

➤ *List the services and benefits you have because taxpayers have financed it, starting with your education; then estimate what each of these services is worth.*

➤ *Write a prayer of thanksgiving.*

➤ *Write a pledge of solidarity, i.e., what you will do to carry out your "duty of solidarity."*

GLOBAL INTERDEPENDENCE IS A DAILY REALITY

Consider this passage from Martin Luther King, Jr.'s final Christmas sermon on peace:

. . . All life is interrelated. We are all caught in an inescapable network of mutuality, tied into a single garment of destiny. Whatever affects one directly, affects all indirectly. We are made to live together because of the interrelated structure of reality. Did you ever stop to think that you can't leave for your job in the morning without being dependent on most of the world? You get up in the morning and go to the bathroom and reach over for the sponge, and that's handed to you by a Pacific Islander. You reach for a bar of soap, and that's given to you at the hands of a Frenchman. And then you go into the kitchen to drink your coffee for the morning, and that's poured into your cup by a South American. And maybe you want tea: that's poured into your cup by a Chinese. Or maybe you're desirous to having cocoa for breakfast, and that's poured into your cup by a West African. And then you reach over for your toast, and that's given to you at the hands of an English-speaking farmer, not to mention the baker. Before you finish eating breakfast in the morning, you've depended on more than half of the world. This is the way our universe is structured, this is its interrelated quality. We aren't going to have peace on earth until we recognize this basic fact of the interrelated structure of all reality (quoted in A Testament of Hope: The Essential Writings and Speeches of Martin Luther King, Jr., *p. 254).*

➤ *Make a list of all the goods and services you use in the course of your day that come from other parts of the world. Start with these categories and see how many items you can name with the possible countries of origin for each.*

Food

Clothing

Transportation

Electronic Products and Services

Recreational Items

Plastic, Aluminum, and Paper Products

Chapter 3, Activity 2

The Common Good and the Family

Step 1—Introduction

This activity expands on the segments in the Student Text on the common good (pages 59–63) and family (pages 67–68). Since the handouts in this activity invite discussion with their families, the three steps might best be done over a period of three weeks, one step for each week.

Step 2—Family meetings

Discussion

Distribute the handout "Principles for Family Meetings" (page 60) and ask students who have had some experience at home with family meetings to describe how they were conducted, the impact the meetings have on their families, their own thoughts and feelings about the process, and their recommendations for other families. Ask other students what they think would be the biggest obstacles to doing family meetings in their own homes and brainstorm ways to overcome these obstacles.

Experiment at home with family meetings

Encourage students to bring their student handout home and discuss the possibility of trying family meetings with the other members of their family.

Step 3—Serving the common good by sharing family tasks

Reflection

Distribute the handout "Two Family Meeting Agenda Items" (page 61) and focus on the first item—serving the common good within your family. Invite students to write their answers to the first three questions.

Discussion

Invite students to compare their answers in pairs. Next, discuss as a whole group what the students learned about themselves and their families in answering these questions. Focus on the fourth question and brainstorm ways to promote fuller participation by all family members in serving the common good of their families.

Reflection

Invite each student to answer the fourth question with regard to their own family.

Discussion, role-play, and decision

Ask students what they think would be the biggest obstacles to bringing this handout home and discussing it with their whole family. You might create a role-play between a student and his or her parents as a way of identifying these obstacles and brainstorming ways to overcome them. Encourage each student to decide whether, how, and when to raise this issue with his or her own family.

Step 4—Serving the common good through family service

Introduction

Start this step by referring to a family's "right to exercise its social and political function in the construction of society"(page 68 of the Student Text). Point out that with every right comes a responsibility. In this case, the corresponding responsibility is to exercise this right and promote the common good of society. It is not just individuals, religious communities, parishes, and schools that have a social mission. Families have a social mission as well.

Reflection

Focus on the second item on the handout—serving the common good of your community and world as a family—and ask students to answer the first question, perhaps sharing their answers in groups of two or three.

Discussion and role-play

Read and discuss the guidelines for family service, one guideline at a time. Ask students what they think would be the biggest obstacles to bringing this agenda item home and discussing it with their whole family. Again, you might create a role-play between a student and his or her parents as a way of identifying these obstacles and brainstorming ways to overcome them.

Discussion

Starting with the list of "15 Things You Can Do for the Poor" (page 63 in the Student Text), brainstorm ways that families can be of service in their community or world.

Reflection and decision

Ask students to focus on the last question and identify what they think their family could do. Then encourage each student to decide whether, how, and when to raise this issue with their own family.

PRINCIPLES FOR FAMILY MEETINGS

REGULARLY SCHEDULED. *After an initial trial, schedule them regularly, so that there is some predictability.*

CONVENIENT FOR ALL. *Schedule them for the most convenient time for all involved. Length is determined by the ages of the family members and how much needs to be discussed.*

QUALITY VS. QUANTITY. *Don't try to finish all the items on the agenda for a particular meeting if some items are taking more time than anticipated. Carry the less urgent items over to the next meeting, if necessary.*

MAKE THE AGENDA AVAILABLE TO EVERYONE. *Have a piece of paper posted where all family members can see it and add whatever items they want discussed.*

PLANS AS WELL AS PROBLEMS. *Make sure that agenda items include family plans, family fun events, and family service. Don't limit the agenda only to problems or conflicts.*

CLEAR RULES AND EVERYONE HAS A CHANCE TO SPEAK. *Establish a set of rules that everyone agrees to; e.g., no one speaks a second time on an item until everyone has a chance to speak, raise your hand if you want to speak, no name calling, etc.*

BRAINSTORM ALTERNATIVES BEFORE DECIDING. *Don't always settle on the first solution proposed. Don't criticize brainstormed possibilities right away. Identify a number of possible solutions and then evaluate each one.*

DECIDE BY CONSENSUS. *Voting usually means some win and some lose. If at all possible, choose a solution that everyone is at least willing to try for a short time, even if they aren't sure it will work. If you can't reach a consensus, carry the item over to the next meeting.*

ROTATE LEADERSHIP. *This helps to develop everyone's leadership skills and creates a greater sense of equality.*

TREATS. *Combine family meetings with things that people enjoy—a food treat, music, a pleasant environment, a favorite game.*

CLEAR AND WRITTEN DECISIONS. *Be sure that the decisions are clear, tasks are assigned, consequences are identified when necessary, and that a check-in time is identified (i.e., a time to evaluate how well a particular solution is working).*

AFFIRMATIONS AND PRAYER. *Consider starting your family meetings with some kind of affirmation of one another—e.g., each person sharing one good thing or one difficult thing that happened that day or week, with other family members expressing encouragement. Consider concluding with a prayer of gratitude for being family and a prayer to be faithful to the decisions made.*

TWO FAMILY MEETING AGENDA ITEMS

1. Serving the common good within your family

➤ List the benefits from being a member of your family.

➤ List the responsibilities that come with these benefits.

➤ How are the tasks and responsibilities in your family shared by all?

➤ What could your family do to share these more equitably, so that every family member contributes to the common good according to their abilities?

2. Serving the common good of your community and world as a family

➤ How does your family already serve the common good (e.g., donate to those in need, organize neighborhood events, participate in community or parish service opportunities)?

Some guidelines for family service

- Invite, but don't force, all family members to participate.

- Choose projects that everyone can participate in in some way.

- Choose projects where you get to meet and work side-by-side with those who are the recipients of the service.

- Add a social change dimension to the service whenever possible; e.g., a family letter to local or national political leaders on behalf of those served.

- Whenever possible, integrate service with faith—doing service during Lent or Advent and combining the service with reflection and prayer.

- Consider doing the service with another family or with special friends of the children.

- Combine the service with some kind of treat—ice cream or a picnic afterward.

- Put "family service" on your family meeting agenda at least once a month and have everyone decide what to do and how to do it.

➤ What could your whole family do in the next week/month to be of service to the community or world?

Chapter 3, Activity 3

The Common Good
of the Last Should Be First

Step 1—Introduction

This activity focuses on the common good and the preferential option for the poor (see pages 59–63 of the Student Text), on the reality of "permissible victims" and "disposable people" in our communities, nation, and world. It serves as the transition activity to Chapter 4 on the dignity of every human life.

Step 2—Scripture and Church teaching

Reflection

Read aloud the entire parable of the rich man and Lazarus (Luke 16:19–31). Distribute the handout "Permissible Victims and Disposable People" (page 65) and reread the opening verses of the parable. Invite students to think about the first question: "What is Jesus saying to you through this parable?" Invite them to share their answers in groups of two or three or as a whole group.

Discussion

Brainstorm answers to the next two questions with the group:

- Who are the people who look the most like Lazarus in our world today?

- Where are such people most likely to be found?

If students have trouble identifying such people, add some categories yourself—e.g., criminals, people with AIDS, homeless men, homeless men of color, single mothers with more than two children, single mothers of color with more than two children, men cleaning toilets at rest stops on Interstate highways, severely deformed people. . . .

Continuum

As a more engaging way to reflect on and discuss the next question—"How does society think of and act toward such people?"—create a continuum from "totally rejected" to "tolerated." If space permits, put "totally rejected" as far to one side of the room as possible and "tolerated" as far to the other side as possible. Identify each group of persons named in the earlier questions, one at a time, and ask students to get up from their seats and place themselves on the continuum reflecting how they think society treats that group. You might add other descriptors to some of the groups and see if that changes students' positions on the continuum. For instance, to the group "people with AIDS," you might add, "African Americans with AIDS."

Discussion

Before asking the last question about the label of "permissible victims" and "disposable people," ask students what these phrases mean to them. Fr. Bryan Massingale, a theologian and an expert on racism, uses these phrases to describe those people whom our society has largely written off—especially people of color who are poor.

Research

As a way of testing students' sense of who are "permissible victims" and "disposable people," ask students to research the questions/issues in segment 2 of the handout. Encourage them to bring news stories and photographs of some of the "permissible victims" and "disposable people" in our communities, nation, and world.

Step 3—Applying this teaching to our own lives

Discussion

Brainstorm responses to the first question in segment 3 of the handout about who these people are in your own community and state.

Reflection and/or continuum

Invite students to reflect in writing on the next two questions about how close these people are to the students' homes and how the students think of and act toward such people. If the continuum worked well in step 2, you might use it here for the third question, though it would require students to show publicly how they regard such people.

Discussion

Read aloud the whole quotation from the Second Vatican Council from page 60 of the Student Text, and then reread the segment quoted on the handout. Discuss what the phrase "every person without exception" implies for them. Discuss the various ways people can "come across our paths" and how to expand the paths of our lives.

Discussion

Referring to the material on the "preferential option for the poor" (pages 62–63 of the Student Text), and to Jesus' frequent teaching that it is the "least" of his people who are special in the eyes of God, discuss what it means to make someone who is "last" on society's list of people who matter be "first" on our list of people who matter. In what specific ways can we make the "option" for them?

Reflection and decision

Invite students to respond in writing to the last three questions. If time permits, ask them to share their reflections and decisions in groups of two or three.

PERMISSIBLE VICTIMS AND DISPOSABLE PEOPLE

1. Consider this parable of Jesus:

"There was a rich man who dressed in purple garments and fine linen and dined sumptuously each day. And lying at his door was a poor man named Lazarus, covered with sores, who would gladly have eaten his fill of the scraps that fell from the rich man's table. Dogs even used to come and lick his sores" (Luke 16:19–22).

➤ *What is Jesus saying to you through this parable?*

➤ *Who are the people in our world today who look the most like Lazarus?*

➤ *Where are such people most likely to be found?*

➤ *How does society think of and act toward those people?*

➤ *Would the label "permissible victims" or "disposable people" be an accurate description of society's attitudes toward such people? Why or why not?*

2. Research the realities:

• *Who gets to go to the best schools? the top priority for job openings? the longest prison terms?*

• *Who are people who get the most minimum-wage jobs?*

• *In which areas are toxic wastes often dumped?*

• *When a company is forced to make cuts, who is most at jeopardy to have their wages/salaries cut or positions terminated?*

• *When state and federal budget cuts are made, programs benefiting what groups are usually cut first?*

• *Who gets first consideration in disasters? For example, compare the U.S. government's initial response to the victims of 9/11 and to the victims of Hurricane Katrina. Do "permissible victims" have anything to do with this difference?*

3. Reflect and decide:

➤ *Who are the "permissible victims" and "disposable people" in your own community or state?*

➤ *How close to the door of your house do you find them?*

➤ *How do you think of and act toward such people?*

➤ *Consider these words from the Second Vatican Council:*

". . . So as not to imitate the rich man who had no concern for the poor man Lazarus, in our times a special obligation binds us to make ourselves the neighbor of every person without exception, and of actively helping him [her] when he [she] comes across our path . . . " (page 60 in your text).

➤ *Do such people regularly or occasionally cross your path? If so, how have you responded in the past? What will you do the next time?*

➤ *If they don't cross your path, how can you invite them in and/or enlarge your paths—the paths of your mind (what you read, view, discuss) as well as the paths you walk or ride.*

➤ *Who among society's "disposable people" will be first on your list of people who matter? What will you do to turn this option or decision into deeds?*

Chapter 4

Justice and the Right to Life

(See pages 75–99 of *Catholic Social Teaching*)

The "seamless garment" theory of a consistent ethic of life in which human life and dignity is affirmed, respected, and protected from "womb to tomb," is presented in these activities. Abortion, euthanasia, and capital punishment are the three life issues addressed in this chapter.

Chapter 4, Activity 1

Promoting Alternatives to Abortion

Step 1—Introduction

This activity is designed to develop a sense of compassion for those faced with the difficult times of pregnancy. Second, it is designed to increase support for the "seamless garment" approach to pro-life activities and for alternatives to abortion, especially adoption and other pro-family public policies, as a strategy for reducing abortions. It builds on the segments in the Student Text on the "Seamless Garment" (pages 94–96), on "There Are Always Alternatives to Abortion" (pages 80–82), and on the pro-life recommendations of the U.S. Bishops (page 82).

Step 2—Compassion for those faced with these difficult decisions

Discussion

Ask students to identify the various kinds of situations in which abortion is seen as an option. Then ask them to choose the one(s) that they would personally find the most challenging and talk about what they think it might be like to "be in the shoes" of someone in that situation.

Reflection and decision

Ask students what it is like to be a student in this school and to be involved in a pregnancy (this includes the boys). In some cases, students feel a sense of being isolated and judged by their peers and adults, as well as their own families. Ask students whether such feelings might increase the tendency of such students to consider abortion. Then ask students whether any changes are needed in their school to create a more supportive environment for those involved in a pregnancy. If so, invite them to make a decision about promoting one of these changes.

Step 3—The "seamless garment" approach

Discussion

Read or summarize the segment in the Student Text (pages 94–96) on the "Seamless Garment," and discuss its meaning and implications for how we are to think and act on issues like abortion. Ask students to identify all of the pro-life activities they are aware of that are currently taking place in their parish and their diocese. Then compare this list with the text's perspective on the "seamless garment."

Research

Encourage students to contact a parish pro-life committee and inquire about the range of pro-life issues they are addressing, what they are specifically doing about each of them, and how they would evaluate their efforts. Consider inviting someone from the pro-life office of the diocese to speak to the class. If this isn't possible, encourage at least one of the students to contact the diocesan office with the same questions.

Discussion

Ask students to share the findings of their research and discuss how much these findings reflect the "seamless garment." Ask students to evaluate the effectiveness of a single-issue approach vs. the "seamless garment" approach. Some points to keep in mind in this discussion:

- The single-issue approach makes it difficult for potential allies who have a wider range of concerns to join them.

- The need to be consistent and comprehensive for life in all stages from conception to natural death.

- The judgmental and unsupportive tone that emerges when, on the one hand, a person tells someone struggling with a difficult pregnancy situation that "the child is innocent, and it's wrong to kill him/her," yet on the other hand judges the person as being irresponsible about sexual behavior and/or fails to ask how they can support the person in making this difficult decision.

Step 4—Pro-family public policy components

Discussion of the causes

In the segment on the two major factors contributing to the disrespect for the sanctity of life, pages 78–79, the Student Text identifies the breakdown of the family as the first factor and offers two causes—the widespread devaluing of responsibility and commitment, and lax laws on divorce. First, ask students if they sense a difference in attitudes about responsibility and commitment between their grandparents' generation, their parents' generation, and their own generation, and why. Then ask students to identify other major factors in the breakdown of the family and other pressures on families that might contribute to abortion; e.g., domestic abuse and poverty.

Discussion of the remedies

Eight pro-life activities that the U.S. bishops ask us to promote as part of our Christian responsibility are listed on page 82 of the Student Text. Read them over as a group, clarify their meaning, and then ask students to identify any other measures that would be helpful in reducing the perceived need for abortion. With regard to the first recommendation, be sure to discuss what other forms of material assistance would be critical, especially for low-income mothers—e.g., available health care, a living wage, childcare, etc.

Research

To determine how widely these recommendations are available in their own community, including their parish and school, and what students can do to promote them, you might assign research teams to each recommendation, plus any others they identified. Because number 2 and number 8 might be difficult to research, you might skip them. Ask each team to contact at least one person or agency (including their parish and school, if appropriate) involved in their recommendation and ask about how available their service/assistance is, what needs to be done to make their work more effective, and how students can help them.

Decision

After the research teams report their findings, encourage the students to choose one thing they will do to help promote the needed services/assistance in their community.

Step 5—The alternative of adoption

Introduction

Of all the alternatives for abortion and the eight recommended pro-life activities, adoption would probably be the most likely one to touch the lives of your students. It is certainly a major life option for married couples and some single people as well.

Reflection and discussion

Distribute the handout "Consider Adoption" (page 72) and ask students to read it carefully and write their answers to the questions that follow. Discuss the first question as a whole group.

Speakers and possible interviews

Invite an adoptive parent, and possibly also an adopted child, to speak to your class. If any of your students are adopted and are comfortable talking about their experience, you might also invite them to share their experience of living in an adoptive family. As a possible follow-up option, assign student teams to contact and interview other adoptive families, focusing on the key issues and questions that emerged from the in-class speaker(s).

Consider Adoption

Their story

"It was in 1969, two years after we were married, that we discovered we couldn't conceive a child. That was a devastating moment, but we knew there was an alternative way to become parents. While we didn't know anyone who was adopted or who had adopted children, we really believed that God wanted us to be parents, so we began the process. In those days, it wasn't nearly as long a wait nor as expensive as it is today. The 'home study' that Catholic Charities conducted with us wasn't difficult and the fact that we didn't make much money didn't stop them from approving us.

"Nine months later, our infant son arrived. When he was two years old, we adopted our second infant son. Eighteen months later, Catholic Charities asked if we would take an infant girl whose birth father was African American and whose birth mother was Native American. Because we lived in a racially integrated neighborhood and had a number of African American and Native American friends and colleagues, we decided that we had the resources to raise our daughter to appreciate both of her racial heritages.

"Over the years, we met many other adoptive families, were part of an interracial family support group, and moved to an even more racially integrated community. The children all went to predominantly African American schools, K–12. We encountered some initial resistance within our own families and an occasional racist comment in public, but for the most part the children were quite comfortable and proud to be part of an interracial family.

"What was really challenging was the children's search for their birth parents. The oldest found his birth mother without any difficulty at age twenty-three because his mother wanted to meet and establish a relationship with him. But he just wanted to know who she was and something about her family history and what he might have inherited genetically from her and his birth father. It was much more difficult for our second son to find his birth mother, but when he did, she quickly became an important part of his life (and ours). Months later, he learned that his birth father was her husband and that they had four other children after they got married. So he had an intact birth family. Thank God we all were sensitive to one another and have become friends. Partly because of the turmoil in that experience, our daughter hasn't sought out her birth parents.

"Would we do it again? Without hesitation. Was it difficult? At times. What do we think about the birth parents? We are so grateful that they chose the painful process of giving birth and then giving their own children to others they hoped would provide a loving home."

Questions

➤ *What would it be like to be an adoptive parent, an adopted child, or a birth parent who gave up a child for adoption?*

➤ *What would be the "pros and cons" for you in considering adoption?*

➤ *Would you be an adoptive parent if the situation pressented itself? Why or why not?*

Chapter 4, Activity 2

Being the Compassion of God for the Dying

Step 1—Introduction

This activity is designed to provide insight and experience into how we can assist dying people to embrace their death in dignity. It challenges us to provide the mercy and dignity that every child of God deserves, especially at their moments of greatest suffering. From the phrases used for euthanasia—"right to die," "death with dignity," and "mercy killing"—this activity extracts their positive elements—"right," "dignity," and "mercy." It is these three words that form the third option offered by the Student Text—compassion for the dying (page 87). Our compassionate God calls us to live out Pope John Paul II's message that "true compassion leads to sharing another's pain . . ." (page 87).

Step 2—The example of Mother Teresa

Reading and research

Have the students return to Chapter 1 of the Student Text and read the sketch of Mother Teresa (pages 24–25). If possible ask students to show a video or photo of Mother Teresa working with the dying in Calcutta. If someone in your community has worked in one of her houses for the dying, invite that person to share their experience.

Discussion

Ask students what would motivate someone to work with destitute people who are dying. Discuss what good that kind of compassion can do for those who are dying and what it says about their dignity as children of God. Ask students what it is that they admire the most about Mother Teresa. Then ask students to write their reflections to question 1 on the handout "Being the Compassion of God" (page 76).

Step 3—The experience of aging family members

Interviews

Encourage students to talk with the oldest members of their extended family about what are the hardest things about growing old and facing death and about how young people can assist them at these difficult times (questions 2 and 3 on the handout). Ask them to write their answers to these questions after the interview(s).

Discussion

Invite students to share what they learned from their interviews, especially about ways that they can be helpful to older people in their final years or months. You might start this sharing in groups of two or three before inviting students to share with the whole group.

Step 4—The experience of nursing homes and hospices

Nursing home observations and interviews

Invite students, perhaps in pairs or with a family member, to visit a local nursing home where they know someone or where your school sends students as part of their community service. Encourage them to observe what is going on, to talk with one or several of the residents and/or someone visiting them and, if possible, with one of the staff about what it's like to be there and how young people could be helpful. Have students write their reflections about this experience on the handout, questions 4 and 5.

Hospice speaker

Invite someone from a local hospice program to speak to your class about what a hospice can do for those who are dying and for their loved ones. Be sure to have them speak about how young people can be helpful to those who are dying and about whether there are volunteer opportunities for high school youth. Some hospice programs involve youth in video recording the stories of those in hospice who want to share their life story with others. Afterward, ask students to write their answer to question 6 on the handout. If time permits, invite them to share their answers with the class.

Step 5—Personal decisions and prayer

Discussion

Encourage students to share what they have learned from this project and what they are thinking they will do or might do to assist someone who is dying and/or the dying person's loved ones.

Decision

Invite students to make a personal decision about what they will do to be the compassion of God for someone who is dying and write their decision in item 7 on the handout.

Prayer

Say together the first verse of the prayer of Mother Teresa from the Student Text, page 27: "Dearest Lord, may I see you today and every day in the person of your sick, and, while nursing them, minister unto you." Invite the students to add their own spontaneous prayers.

BEING THE COMPASSION OF GOD

Use separate sheets of paper for one or more of these items.

1. What did you learn from Mother Teresa about the compassion of God and about how you can be the compassion of God for those who are sick or dying?

2. What did you learn from elderly or sick members of your family about the difficulties of growing old and facing death?

3. What suggestions did they make about how you could be helpful to them? Which suggestions seem like things you could see yourself doing? Which ones didn't seem possible? Why?

4. What did you observe or learn in the nursing home about the difficulties that dying people face?

5. What did you learn about how you could be helpful to people in a setting like that?

6. What did you like about hospice's approach to working with people who are dying? Could you see yourself helping in some way? Why or why not?

7. Out of all the possibilities that emerged during these investigations and reflections, what is one step you can take to be the compassion of God for someone who is elderly or dying?

8. Write a short prayer to God in response to what you have learned and have decided to do or are thinking about doing.

Chapter 4, Activity 3

Capital Punishment Is Not the Way of Jesus

Step 1—Introduction

This activity is designed to help students see the dignity and reflection of God in our society's most "disposable people," those who are incarcerated and especially those on death row, and find ways that they can extend the compassion of God—"be the face of Christ"—to such people. This activity builds on Student Text section "Breaking the Cycle of Violence" (pages 91–92). Step 3 on the "Residents Encounter Christ" prison retreat program is an inspiring invitation to see the face of Christ in incarcerated men and women, but it is labeled "optional," depending on how much time you can give this activity.

Step 2—"Disposable People" and "The Face of Christ"

Photo reflection and discussion

Ask students to look carefully at the photo of the man's hand from the jail cell on page 89 of the Student Text and share the feelings they experience as they look at the photo. You might also brainstorm as a group what they think his life might have been to bring him to this moment. This would surface lots of attitudes which might be useful to know in working through this activity and in subsequent chapters. Finally, discuss society's attitudes toward incarcerated persons, especially those on death row, and whether the label "disposable people" would be appropriate.

Reading and discussion

Summarize the information in "Breaking the Cycle of Violence" on pages 91–92 of the Student Text. Mention the ministry of Sr. Helen Prejan and the movie *Dead Man Walking.* Invite students to share their thoughts or ask questions about Sr. Helen's ministry. Finally, ask students to answer the question she poses —"We ask, 'Don't they deserve to die?' But the real question should be, 'Do we deserve to kill them?'"

Reflection and discussion

Distribute the student handout "Stories of Compassion and Forgiveness" (page 81) and ask students to read "The Story of Sr. Helen Prejean." Have them answer the questions in writing, perhaps sharing them in groups of two or three before discussing them as a whole class. As part of this discussion about how Jesus would regard such people, note that visiting those in prison is one of the seven corporal works of mercy that Jesus identified in Matthew 25:31–46.

Step 3 (Optional)—"Residents Encounter Christ" (REC)

Background

REC is a three-day retreat experience conducted by a group of ten to twenty prison volunteers ("outmates") for a group of twenty to forty prison "inmates." It is an experience of the lavishness of God's love for these men and women who are in a situation of real deprivation. There are short presentations by both outmates and inmates, plus small group discussions on death, resurrection, and being sent forth ("Die Day, Rise Day, and Go Day") paralleling the Paschal mystery of Christ and applied to life in prison. Much of the lavishness comes through dozens of donuts and cookies during breaks, a real banquet feast with china and silver, a foot-washing service, and testimonies from both outmates and inmates on the healing love of God in their lives. Lives are profoundly touched by these REC weekends and the monthly follow-up fellowship evenings.

Reflection and discussion

Sr. Helen Prejean's profound statement to Patrick—"I will be the face of Christ for you"—and its challenge to us to be the same for other "disposable people" focuses on our being Christ for them. (*Note:* The character in the movie version of *Dead Man Walking* is named Matthew.) The title of the REC program is also accurate; prison "residents" truly encounter Christ in the love of the outmates. But it's the converse that is equally important. Sr. Helen and the REC volunteers truly encounter Christ in those incarcerated men and women. They are the "face of Christ for us."

Story and discussion

Tell students this story of one REC experience and ask for their reactions and what it says to them about the special love of God for those society deems "disposable people."

> *It was Christmas night, 1995, the fourth Wednesday of the month and therefore an REC fellowship gathering of outmates and inmates at this Missouri prison. Not all outmates were able to leave their families that night, but the ones who did will never forget the experience. It was a clear, crisp evening with a sky full of stars. The closer the outmates got to the prison, the brighter the stars seemed to get. It almost seemed as if the stars came to a stop right over the prison. As they walked across the prison yard, they continued to stare at the bright night sky above. Once the gathering began and the Scriptures were read, more than one person had a sense of the presence of God that seemed more tangible than usual. One person shared that the experience reminded him of the Magi coming to find the Christ child. By the end of the evening, it was clear that the outmates had indeed found Jesus—in the lives of their incarcerated brothers in faith.*

Ask: "How was the experience of the outmates similar to the experience of the magi?"

Step 4—The story of Bud Welch

Reflection and discussion

Ask students to read the story of Bud Welch on the student handout "Stories of Compassion and Forgiveness" (page 81). Supplement this short profile and statement with information about Bud Welch and his efforts to abolish capital punishment. See www.journeyofhope.org. Invite the students to write their answers to the two questions following the passage and then discuss these questions as a whole group.

Reflection and discussion

Explain that the photo on page 81 is of a cross that hung on the chain-link fence surrounding the bombsite in Oklahoma City for several years and was then placed in the museum next to the bombsite. Ask students to look silently at the photo and then reflect in writing what it says to them. Invite them to share their reflections either in small groups or as a whole group.

Step 5—Responding to the needs of these "disposable people"

Discussion

Distribute the student handout "Your Own Response" (page 82) and read through it together with the students, clarifying the various action possibilities in each category and adding other possibilities that you or the students know of. Identify those that seem most feasible for your community or diocese and especially if what the students at St. Louis University High School did could be adapted for your own school.

Decision and planning

Encourage students to identify one or two of these action possibilities that they would like to pursue further. Invite students to name their selection(s) and see if there is more than one person interested in the same options. Invite those students interested in the same options to discuss whether they would like to work together. Encourage those who want to act, whether as individuals or in teams, to begin planning their next steps.

STORIES OF COMPASSION AND FORGIVENESS

The story of Sr. Helen Prejean

In the book Dead Man Walking, Sr. Helen tells us about her visit with Patrick the day before his execution, when she asks him if he would like her to be present in the observation room to witness his execution. When he says yes, she tells him that at that last moment he should look into her eyes and she would be "the face of Christ for you." She would be the eyes of Jesus looking lovingly and forgivingly at him at that ultimate moment.

➤ Do you think Patrick deserved such love? Why or why not?

➤ What do you think of Sr. Helen's ministry? Could you see yourself as an adult doing anything like it? Why or why not?

The story of Bud Welch

The cross of Jesus imaged on the chain-link fence surrounding the bombsite in Oklahoma City speaks volumes—"168 Reasons to Love One Another." While many in Oklahoma City and around the United States wanted the death penalty for Timothy McVeigh, others rose above their pain and rage and heard the words of Jesus: "Father, forgive them, for they know not what they do."

Bud Welch was one of those courageous people of faith who reached out to the father of Timothy McVeigh and then to Timothy himself. What made this gesture of reconciliation so profound was that Bud's twenty-three-year-old daughter Julie was one of those 168 victims. It took nine months of anger and rage, which almost destroyed Bud's soul, before he found the love and courage to do as Jesus did. But he did. In his own words—

> I was opposed to the death penalty all my life until my daughter Julie Marie was killed in the Oklahoma City bombing. For many months after the bombing I could have killed Timothy McVeigh myself. Temporary insanity is real, and I have lived it. You can't think of enough adjectives to describe the rage, revenge, and hate I felt. But after time, I was able to examine my conscience, and I realized that if McVeigh is put to death, it won't help me in the healing process. People talk about executions bringing closure. But how can there be closure when my little girl is never coming back? I finally realized that the death penalty is all about revenge and hate, and revenge and hate are why Julie Marie and 167 others are dead.

➤ How would you have felt if you were in Bud's situation? Do you agree with his realization that "the death penalty is all about revenge and hate . . ."? Why or why not?

➤ Why do you think Bud reached out to Timothy's father and then to Timothy himself?

➤ What might you have done in the same situation?

YOUR OWN RESPONSE

Learn more

- *Read or see* Dead Man Walking.

- *Contact Catholics Against Capital Punishment (www.cacp.org) and ask for a copy of their newsletter.*

- *Contact the criminal justice ministry office in your diocese or parish and find out what they do and how you might be able to help.*

- *Search the Internet under "Victim Offender Reconciliation Program" and see if there is a group in your area. For a Directory of Victim Offender Mediation Programs in the United States, go to www.ojp.gov/ovc/publications/infores/restorative_justice.*

Donate and/or volunteer

- *Donate books and magazines to your Criminal Justice Ministry Office or other local prison ministry offices. They will give these to inmates and prison libraries.*

- *Donate toys and other Christmas gifts to agencies working with children whose parents are incarcerated.*

- *Volunteer at one of these agencies.*

Vigil, pray, and organize against capital punishment

Students at St. Louis University High School in St. Louis began their campaign against capital punishment in May 2005, shortly after the release of the U.S. Bishops' statement on capital punishment. With the help of a teacher, several members of the Amnesty International chapter decided to write a letter to the Governor of Missouri protesting the establishment of death row at a newer correctional center in Bonne Terre, Missouri, where the men would be cut off from their inmate support network. Students posted a flyer at school and the photo of the next person scheduled for execution and collected three pages of signatures to their letter. Over the next four months, Missouri executed three men. The night before each execution, several students and at least one parent joined a prayer vigil in a central location in St. Louis. One student and his mother even traveled the seventy-five miles to Bonne Terre to join the prayer vigil outside the prison. This case was especially tragic because the convicted man had killed his grandmother, but the extended family pleaded in vain with the Governor to commute his sentence. They had suffered enough.

This core group of four high school juniors was determined to increase student awareness about capital punishment and to engage more students in the prayer vigils. They invite you to consider these possibilities, especially if you are in a state that continues to use the death penalty:

- *Join a vigil on the evening of an execution and pray for the person to be executed, for the families of their victims, and for an end to capital punishment in your state.*

- *Request or organize a school prayer service or a prayer over the intercom on the day of an execution.*

- *Encourage your school or parish liturgy committee to include a Prayer of the Faithful on behalf of those executed by the state—on Respect Life Sunday, Good Friday, and other times when petitions are spoken about respect for all human life.*

Chapter 5

Justice and Prejudice

(See pages 101–123 of *Catholic Social Teaching*)

Prejudice is the source of many injustices. When it threatens the rights of people, exhibits stereotypical thinking, and when it resists new information about people, negative prejudice turns sinful. Sinful prejudice manifests itself in hatred of homosexual persons, anti-Semitism, ageism, and sexism, among other forms of bigotry.

Chapter 5, Activity 1

Your Own Experiences with Prejudice

Step 1—Introduction

Before addressing the issue of racism in Chapter 6, this chapter focuses on prejudice in general. This activity is designed to help students personalize the issue of prejudice, starting with their own experiences of being on the receiving end of prejudice. This is the prelude to their examining their own prejudices and then deciding how to change.

Steps 2 and 3 build on the "Real-Life Prejudice" (pages 103–107) and the "Stages of Prejudice" (pages 108–116) in the Student Text. Step 4 is based on the "Nine Ways You Can Fight Prejudice" (page 116) in the Student Text.

Step 2—Being victims of prejudice

Reflection and sharing

Distribute the handout "Your Own Experiences With Prejudice" (page 87) and ask students to write their answers to the questions under "How have you been the victim of prejudice?" If the students are comfortable with small group sharing, you might have them share their answers in groups of two or three before a general class discussion.

Depending on time, you could solicit their answers to the first four questions before focusing on "How does it feel to be the victim of prejudice?" This is the key question.

Step 3—Observing others being victims of prejudice

Reflection and sharing

Perhaps referring students back to the examples in their text under "Real-Life Prejudice" (pages 103–107), ask students to write their answers to the questions under "What forms of prejudice have you observed? And where?" Again, if the students are comfortable with small group sharing and time permits, you might have them share their answers in groups of two or three before a class discussion.

Discussion

Focus the discussion primarily on the second and third questions, since these can lead to greater empathy and courage.

Step 4—Your own prejudices

Reflection and sharing

Ask students to write their answers to the questions under "How serious are your own prejudices toward other people?" Be sure to point out the "other" category in the list of groups. It may also be helpful to brainstorm ways we exclude people. Continue with the same process of discussion as before.

Discussion

Focus the discussion primarily on the questions "With which group of people are you the most uncomfortable as well as prejudiced? Why?"

Step 5—Decision and action plan

Discussion

Brainstorm ways that students can change their discomforts and prejudices. You might include an actual example of your own prejudice as an illustration of going to those people about whom you have a prejudice and listening to their life experience in an open, nonjudgmental manner. Evaluate the pros and cons of such a strategy and how to do it respectfully. Be sure to also include the examples in "Nine Ways You Can Fight Prejudice" (page 116 of the Student Text).

Decision

Encourage students to answer the last question on the student handout and then begin to map out a strategy for implementing the decision.

Step 6—Prayer

Jesus, as a practicing Jew of your time, you were a scandal to many of your Jewish brothers and sisters, especially when you spoke openly and respectfully to the Samaritan woman at the well, when you healed those with leprosy, when you embraced the children, when you defended the woman accused of adultery, when you ate with tax collectors and so-called "sinners," when you healed the servant of an "enemy" Roman officer.

Help us to confront our own prejudices toward such people and toward others in our society. Give us the courage and compassion to reach out across our comfort zones and begin to break down the barriers that keep us from being your "beloved community" where every person is valued as a precious child of God, as one of your sisters and brothers.

YOUR OWN EXPERIENCES WITH PREJUDICE

How have you been the victim of prejudice?

    ➤ *Because of your age? How and when?*

    ➤ *Because of your body shape? How and when?*

    ➤ *Because of your ethnicity or race? How and when?*

    ➤ *Because of your gender? How and when?*

    ➤ *How does it feel to be the victim of prejudice?*

What forms of prejudice have you observed? Where?

    ➤ *Which have been the most prevalent?*

    ➤ *Which bother you the most? Why?*

    ➤ *Did you ever challenge any of this prejudice? Why or why not?*

How serious are your own prejudices toward other people?

On a scale of 1 to 10, with 10 being the most prejudiced, how would you rank your attitudes toward the following groups? Think about hurtful words or phrases have you ever used in talking about each group and write how have you excluded them in your thoughts and actions?

Group	Ranking	Ways you've excluded them
Elderly people		
Women		
People with disabilities		
Gays and lesbians		
Jews		
Muslims		
African Americans		
Hispanic Americans		
Native Americans		
Asian Americans		
European Americans		
Non-English speaking immigrants		
Obese people		
Other: _____		

➤ *With which group of people are you the most uncomfortable as well as prejudiced? Why?*

Decisions

➤ *What can you do to change your discomfort and prejudice? What's your plan for putting this decision into practice?*

Chapter 5, Activity 2

Challenging Sexism in Your Own Life

Step 1—Introduction

In every society, women are the victims of prejudice and abuse. While some aspects of sexism are manifested in the early stages of prejudice (see page 109 of the Student Text), other aspects escalate to the stage of physical attacks (page 112). For youth, this more serious dimension of sexism takes the form of dating violence, which includes verbal and emotional abuse as well as physical attacks. This activity challenges youth to examine seriously this issue of dating violence, as well as the manifestations of sexism in their lives at home, in the culture, and at school. This activity begins with these less serious or more prevalent manifestations before addressing the more serious one. Depending on the length of your class periods and the amount of good discussion generated in step 2, this activity might best be done over two class periods.

It is critical that this issue be discussed in the classroom. Sexual abuse is an issue directly affecting a large percentage of women (and children) and indirectly affecting our entire society.

Step 2—Challenging sexism at home, in the culture, and at school

Reflection

Distribute the student handout "Challenging Sexism in Your Life" (page 93) and ask the students to reflect in writing on the questions under "At home." You might ask for some examples of "men's work" and "women's work" to stimulate their personal reflection.

Discussion and decision

After discussing their answers to the first three questions, invite them to make a decision about their next step in addressing sexism in their own home.

Repeat the process

Have students do the same reflection, discussion, and decision on each of the other two venues—"In the culture" and "At school."

Step 3—Definition and data on dating violence

Statement in the Student Text

Begin with the last statement about sexism in the Student Text (page 109)—"The most serious problem confronting women is how men victimize them with violence through assaults, beatings, and rape." You might ask students to rank themselves on a scale from "strongly agree" to "strongly disagree" and ask for the reasons for their ranking.

Definition of dating violence

Dating violence may be defined as the perpetration or threat of an act of violence by at least one member of an unmarried couple on the other member within the context of dating or courtship. This violence encompasses any form of sexual assault, physical violence, and verbal or emotional abuse.

Some data on dating violence

Summarizing many studies, the average prevalence rate for nonsexual dating violence is 22 percent among male and female high school students and 32 percent among college students. Females are somewhat more likely than males to report being victims of violence. Over half of a representative sample of more than 1,000 female students at a large urban university had experienced some form of unwanted sex—12 percent of these acts were perpetrated by casual dates and 43 percent by steady dating partners.

For more data, contact the National Center for Injury Prevention: www.cdc.gov/ncipc/default.htm.

Discussion

Ask the students whether any of this data surprises them. Why or why not?

Step 4—Consider these case studies

Notes and directions

The two case studies provide an opportunity for students to discuss the issue in less revealing ways before they are asked to address the issue in their own lives. Make sure that the boys deal with the male behavior in each case study and not just what the girl could do. With each case study, you might have students respond to the questions first in groups of two or three, before having a large group discussion. You might consider inviting students to role-play each situation before the discussion.

1. You've had a crush on this guy since your freshman year. Now he's a senior and you're a sophomore and he speaks to you at school. You tell your friends, but they warn you to be careful, that he likes to sleep around. But you really want to go with him, so you do. He tells you how beautiful you are, that he has a condom, and that he would like to "hook up" with you. You're afraid he won't talk to you again if you don't have sex with him. If you were this person, what would you do?

2. In the midst of a conversation with your boyfriend, you tell him you're going out Friday night with your girl friends. He gets upset and says, "What's wrong with going out with me? I had plans for us for Friday night." You complain that he's always calling you to find out where you are, who you're with, and what you're wearing. He really gets mad and hits you. If you were the young woman, what would you do? If you knew this was going on and knew the young man, what would you say or do? If you knew this was going on and knew the young woman, what would you say or do?

Step 5—Challenging dating violence

Background

Before addressing the specific issue of dating violence, focus on other manifestations of sexism in students' relationships with the opposite sex in general.

Brainstorm

Have students refocus on the handout. Before asking students to reflect on their own experiences in these relationships, it would be good to ask for examples of "equal" and "unequal" relationships.

Reflection and sharing

Ask students to answer in writing the questions on "In relationships with the opposite sex in general" and share some of their reflections in groups of two or three, before a whole class reflection and discussion of the first two questions. Then invite students to make a specific decision in answering the third question: "What could you do to change at least one of these unequal aspects?"

Reflection on dating violence

Ask students to reflect in writing on the questions "on dating violence."

Discussion

Encourage students to share their thoughts aloud on several of these questions:
  How does it feel to be the victim of dating violence? *Note:* It is crucial for boys to begin to understand the impact of such violence on girls.
  What can you do when you're in such a situation?
  What can you do or say to others who are in such a situation?
  What could the school do to help in this?

Final reflection

As a way of concluding this difficult exploration, you might ask students to say aloud what they learned from the reflection and discussion of the issue.

CHALLENGING SEXISM IN YOUR LIFE

At home

➤ Are chores and other tasks in your home divided up into "women's work" and "men's work"? How so?

➤ Do you find yourself resistant to breaking out of these stereotypes? If so, why?

➤ Do you think some changes would be beneficial for the whole family? Which and why?

➤ What would be a good first step in making one of these changes?

In the culture

➤ How are women exploited in video games, TV shows and movies, magazines, and advertising? Do you personally participate in or enjoy any of this?

➤ Do you need to do something about any of this? If so, where can you start?

At school

➤ Are there ways in which your school treats young women in unequal or discriminatory ways?

➤ If so, what could you and your classmates, friends, and some teachers do about these?

➤ *What's keeping you from doing something about any of these?*

In your relationships with the opposite sex in general

➤ *In what ways have these relationships been truly equal?*

➤ *In what ways have they been less than equal?*

➤ *What could you do to change at least one of these unequal aspects?*

On dating violence in particular

➤ *Are you (or were you) personally involved in a relationship that is physically, emotionally, or sexually abusive? How did/does it feel?*

➤ *What could you do about it?*

➤ *Are any of your friends involved in abusive relationships? If so, is there something you need to say or do about any of these?*

➤ *Does something need to be done at school to deal with dating violence? What can you do to encourage this?*

Chapter 6

Justice and Racism

(See pages 123–142 of *Catholic Social Teaching*)

Racism is any attitude, action, or institutional structure that subordinates a person or group because of their skin color. This sin of racism attacks the fundamental dignity of human beings, ignoring that each person is a child of God and made in God's image.

Chapter 6, Activity 1

The Realities of Racism

Step 1—Introduction

This activity is designed to help students come to a gut as well as intellectual understanding of some of the realities of racism. It starts with the data and experiences of people of color, challenging white students to be open to some harsh and painful realities and statements.

One of the "realities of racism" that often surfaces in responses is the sense some white Americans have of "reverse racism," as they call it. They may have heard or perhaps even experienced some of the consequences of "affirmative action"—that the preferential treatment that whites took for granted is now being shared with people of color. It's difficult for some white people to accept this, but it must be faced. And for those who are white, facing it means examining the realities of "white privilege." It might be most productive to save the section on "Affirmative Action" (page 129 of the Student Text) for step 4 on "White Privilege," where it can be put in the context of preferential treatment that whites are often unaware of.

Step 2—The statistical realities of racism

Discuss the text

Have students read the particulars of racism for the various groups of people of color in their text, pages 126–136. Ask them which of the statistics surprise them and which disturb them the most.

Supplement the statistics

Use current websites to update the statistics. One excellent source for comparative statistics presented in a way that students understand them is the Children's Defense Fund. Go to their website—www.childrensdefense.org—and click on "Data" and then click on "Moments in America for Children." These lists compare all children, white children, black children, Latino children, Asian children, and American Indian children. Again, ask students to identify those statistics that surprise them and disturb them.

Step 3—The personal realities of racism

Discuss students' own experiences

Invite students of color to share some of their experiences of racism. Ask all students to share instances of racism that they have observed.

Class speaker and/or interviews

As a way of supplementing students' own experiences, especially in a predominantly white school, invite a panel of speakers representing different racial/cultural groups to share their experiences. To involve students more closely in the process, you might also encourage white students to interview at least one person of color and students of color to interview someone from a different racial/cultural group. Ask students to write a report, plus their reflections, on what they learned.

Books and videos

There are many excellent books that help students understand the personal realities of racism. See "Other Resources for Chapter 6 Activities," page 115.

Step 4—The realities of "white privilege"

Discuss "Affirmative Action"

Read the segment on "Affirmative Action" (page 129 of the Student Text) and have the students reflect on the two passages from the U.S. Bishops. Invite white students to share their experiences with what some call "reverse racism." Then ask them to be open in considering the student handout on "White Privilege" (page 99).

Introduce "White Privilege"

Distribute the student handout and introduce it as a way for white students to become more aware of some of the preferential treatment they experience just because they are white. Encourage them to reflect on it with an open mind and heart.

Reading and individual reflection

Ask students to mark each of the twelve items on the handout—a plus sign for items that they agree with, a minus sign by those they disagree with, and a question mark by those they aren't sure about or don't understand. Students of color should mark the items they have experienced in reverse.

Note: For a more engaging approach, put each of the twelve items on index cards and distribute them to students. Ask each student to stand and read their card aloud, perhaps twice for emphasis. If it is a student of color, have them reverse the adjectives from "no one will . . ." to "all or many will. . . ."

Discussion

Take each item, one at a time, and ask how students marked them. Spend additional time discussing those items that generate the most intense responses. Do item 13 as a whole group, perhaps listing those other forms of white privilege on the board or newsprint.

Group reflection

Ask the students as a whole group how they felt as they read the thirteen items. Then brainstorm as a group what white students and adults can do about these white privileges and specific ways they can renounce any of them.

Decision

Invite students to write their answers to the final question, one for white students and the other for students of color.

Prayer

Conclude this activity with a prayer for wisdom and courage.

WHITE PRIVILEGE

1. *I can walk down a residential street in a white neighborhood and no one will automatically think that I am a babysitter or a delivery person.*
2. *If I make any grammatical or spelling errors, no one will attribute my mistakes to my race.*
3. *I can walk into a store late at night and probably no one will think that I am there to rob it.*
4. *In the classroom, it is not automatically assumed that I will have to work harder than others to get good grades.*
5. *Most everyone who looks at me will assume that I am an American citizen and can speak English.*
6. *If I have a responsible job or a scholarship, no one thinks that I got it because of "quotas."*
7. *Other white people in an elevator won't tense up and wonder what I might do.*
8. *I can pay with a credit card or check and won't be questioned.*
9. *People hear that I am going to college and no one is surprised.*
10. *If I want to teach my younger brothers and sisters about my culture, there are many museums and cultural events to which I can take them.*
11. *I can have or wear nice things or ride in a nice car and no one will automatically think that I'm being wasteful or say, "Isn't that typical?"*
12. *No one assumes when I give my opinion that I am speaking on behalf of my entire race.*
13. *What other privileges do white Americans enjoy?*
    (adapted from Kathleen McGinnis, Celebrating Racial Diversity, Institute for Peace and Justice, 2005)

For reflection:

➤ *What were your feelings as you read this?*

➤ **(For white students)** *Which one of these "white privileges" do you need to look at more carefully and what are you going to do about it?*

➤ **(For students of color)** *Which one of these items do you experience as especially hurtful and what could you do to challenge that and do it in a way that might help whites address their privilege?*

Chapter 6, Activity 2

Becoming an Inclusive Christian

Step 1—Introduction

This activity is designed to put the reflection on "Being Inclusive" in the Student Text (pages 137–138) into practice, beginning with how racially inclusive students are at the present moment and proceeding to how they could become more racially inclusive. The two student handouts are adapted from *Celebrating Racial Diversity*, Kathleen McGinnis's manual for teachers, K–12.

Step 2—The inclusivity of Jesus

Read the pertinent Scripture passage on page 137 of the Student Text, plus the first paragraph on page 137 about who Jesus spent time with. Have students share their reflections on the readings, perhaps first in small groups.

Step 3—"Racial Profile"

Questions 1–4

Distribute the handout "Racial Profile" (pages 103–104) and ask students to write their answers to questions 1–4. After they finish, ask them what they learned about themselves from their responses. You might also invite them to share what they learned in small groups.

Questions 5–6

Have students answer questions 5 and 6 as best they can. Then ask for which groups they had a hard time identifying notable persons. Discuss what this says about them and about our society as a whole.

Question 7

Ask students to write their answers, then share them in small groups, and if time allows, in the whole group. This is a key question for considering the decision to follow.

Question 8 and decision

Ask students to complete the handout and then share their decisions in their small groups. Tell them that the next student handout will provide an opportunity to explore further possibilities for change.

Step 4—"A Personal Affirmative Action Program"

Brainstorm possibilities

Distribute the student handout "A Personal Affirmative Action Program" (page 105). Before asking students to make decisions on their own, it will be very helpful to brainstorm possible ways of doing each of the seven elements, one element at a time. List these possibilities on newsprint, so that students can refer to them as they make decisions.

Decisions

It will be easier to ask students to make a tentative decision for each of the seven elements—something they would seriously consider doing. At the completion of the seven elements, ask students to go back over their seven action possibilities and then write their response to the "For reflection and decision" item at the bottom of the page. Again, these could be shared in small groups.

Prayer

Use the "Prayer Reflection" on page 141 of the Student Text to conclude this activity.

Racial Profile

The questions below refer to your own racial experiences and background.
After the questions have been answered, use them as a basis for group discussion.

1. What is the racial composition of the people with whom you go to school now?

2. What is the racial composition of the neighborhood in which you live?

3. What has been the racial character of your educational experiences in the past? (Racial identity of fellow students, teachers, etc.)

4. Have any previous living or working experiences put you in contact with a significant number of people from a racial group other than your own? (If there are many of these experiences, list just the last three.)

5. What notable African American person do you admire the most:

a. in your own area/city

b. on a national scale

6. Answer question 5 in terms of:

• Hispanic (local; national)

• Native American (local; national)

• Asian (local; national)

• *Jewish (local; national)*

• *Caucasian (local; national)*

7. Name one experience that has had a positive impact on your racial attitudes.

8. Using the scale below, how would you assess your own racial experiences/background?

Totally your own race   *Totally multiracial*

| 1 | 2 | 3 | 4 | 5 | 6 | 7 | 8 | 9 | 10 |

➤ *Where would you like to be on that scale five years from now?*

Decision:
➤ *What one thing can you do now to move yourself toward that point?*

(adapted with permission from Kathleen McGinnis, Celebrating Racial Diversity, *Institute for Peace and Justice, 2005)*

A Personal Affirmative Action Program

1. What books, articles, magazines, and issues could I read (about) to deepen my understanding of racism and the positive contributions of people from different racial/cultural groups to my community, nation, and world?

2. What educational experiences and resource persons from different racial/cultural groups could I seek out to break down negative stereotypes as well as deepen my understanding of racism and the positive contributions of people from different racial/cultural groups?

3. What opportunities do I have to seek the services of professionals (doctors, dentists, educators, counselors, social workers, ministers, etc.) from different racial/cultural groups?

4. What opportunities are available to me to encounter people from different racial/cultural groups or experience the values and perspectives of other cultures when I shop, worship, recreate, travel, etc.?

5. How can I better cultivate friendships with people from different racial/cultural groups?

6. In what concrete ways could I make my bedroom, and perhaps other rooms in my home, more multicultural in the visuals on the walls, the reading materials on the tables, the guests I invite in, etc.? What about my school locker?

7. What opportunities are there for me to stand with victims of racism (vigils, city council meetings, correspondence, etc.)?

For reflection and decision:

➤ *Choose one of these elements as your next step in dealing with your personal racism and write how you will specifically act on it in the days ahead.*

Chapter 6, Activity 3

Challenging Institutional Racism

Step 1—Introduction

This activity builds on the sections in the Student Text on "Institutional Racism" (pages 125–126) and "Racism Against Certain Groups" (pages 126–136). First, it challenges students to consider the manifestations of institutional racism with an open mind and heart and to reflect on why the Church urges us to action. Second, it invites students to examine institutional racism in their own community and offers them an opportunity to take action.

As an optional intermediate step, the quotes and challenges from Martin Luther King, Jr., provide a prophetic challenge from a prophet who understood and confronted racism with his whole life. His words and witness need to be considered carefully. For further inspiration and practical examples of action, you might have students read how others have challenged racism. Kathleen McGinnis, in *Celebrating Racial Diversity*, has short profiles of nine racial justice heroes, plus activities and actions based on their lives.

As an optional final step, especially if your class or school has a significant number of white students, you could include the further challenge to white students not just to challenge racism, but to challenge it as allies of people of color.

Step 2—Why we should challenge institutional racism

Read and discuss the realities of institutional racism

Have students read the description of institutional racism on page 125 of the Student Text and ask any clarification questions. If time permits, do the "Case Study: Low Income Housing" (page 126). Have students read the manifestations of institutional racism on particular communities of color (pages 126–136 of the Student Text) and discuss any questions that the reading raises.

Reflect on the Church's teaching

Have students read the passages from *Brothers and Sisters to Us* and *The Church and Racism* (pages 128–129 of the Student Text) about why Christians have a responsibility to confront the sin of racism in its institutional forms. Clarify the passages, if needed, and discuss their implications for youth.

Step 3 (Optional)—How others challenged institutional racism and challenge us

Respond to Dr. King's challenge

Distribute the student handout "Dr. King Challenges Us to Confront Racism" page 110. Read each quote, one at a time, and ask students to reflect in writing to the corresponding "challenge."

Other racial justice heroes

As a way of adding both inspiration and examples for action, have students read the story of Saint Katherine Drexel on page 139 of the Student Text. Also, have the students research information and share on other racial justice heroes.

Step 4—"Examining Our Community"

Share the assumption

Distribute the student handout "Examining Our Community" (pages 111–112) and share this assumption behind the handout: The community in which we live affects our attitudes and behaviors. The more we increase our awareness and the more we generate concrete suggestions for action, the more possibilities there are for our attitudes and behaviors to change.

Review the handout and consider additions

Read over with students the different categories for research. Consider any new categories that you and/or the students might want to add to the list.

Determine assignments and give instructions

Ask for volunteers for each of the categories, making sure that at least one student is researching each category. Encourage, but don't force, those working on the same category to work together. Give students seven to ten days to investigate their category, write up the results of their investigation, identify possible actions to address the racism they found, and follow through on one action.

Student reports

Sharing their efforts and results with the whole class should be an occasion for reflection on the experience, affirmation of their efforts, and prayerful gratitude for the courage and compassion to put their faith into practice.

Step 5 (Optional)—Becoming "white allies" of people of color

Background

One of the dimensions of racism and white privilege is the sense that white people should be in charge. One of the challenges, then, for white people is to place themselves in a supportive role to people of color in efforts to challenge racism (or poverty or any other social issue involving people of color).

Discussion

Present this background reflection and brainstorm with students what it means to be a "white ally" and various ways of being just that.

Specific examples

If possible, have students watch the video *The Long Walk Home*, a fictional account of the Montgomery bus boycott, starring Whoopi Goldberg as the African American maid for a wealthy white woman played by Sissy Spacek. In part, this is the story of how this wealthy white mother renounces some of her white privileges and becomes a "white ally" in the boycott.

Dr. King Challenges Us to Confront Racism

"The problem of race is America's greatest moral dilemma."
—Stride Toward Freedom: The Montgomery Story

Quote:

"For too long the depth of racism in American life has been underestimated. The surgery to extract it is necessarily complex and detailed. As a beginning, it is important to X-ray our history and reveal the full extent of the disease."
—Why We Can't Wait

Challenge:

➤ *Conduct your own "X-ray" of U.S. history and write down what it reveals of racism.*

Racism can destroy nations. Will we let it happen to us?

Quote:

"History has shown that, like a virulent disease germ, racism can grow and destroy nations."
—Where Do We Go From Here: Chaos or Community?

Challenge:

➤ *How could racism destroy our nation? How widespread is the disease at this time?*

Quote:

"The racism of today is real, but the democratic spirit that has always faced it is equally real."
—Where Do We Go From Here: Chaos or Community?

Challenge:

➤ *How strong is the "democratic spirit" in the United States today? Is it willing to seriously tackle racism? Why or why not? How willing are you to seriously tackle racism?*

Quote:

"We will have to repent in this generation not merely for the vitriolic words and actions of the bad people, but for the appalling silence of the good people."
—"Letter from Birmingham Jail."

Challenge:

➤ *Have you been part of "the appalling silence of the good people" in the face of racism and other forms of injustice? What can you do to break your silence?*

EXAMINING OUR COMMUNITY

1. Printed Advertising in the Home or Classroom

➤ Make a collage of the sample advertising images in a given magazine. Be sure to include magazines like Ebony, Jet, Hispanic. In what roles are people of color portrayed in the advertising? Where are they pictured in the physical layout? Approximately what percentage of advertising images do they represent? Are stereotypes reinforced? Are there any ads that are particularly good? What makes them good?

- Write a letter to the advertising division of a magazine or corporation explaining your views if you think its advertising should be improved, or is particularly good.

2. Greeting Cards

➤ Check for availability of greeting cards bearing African American, Hispanic, Native American, or Asian images. (Be sure to note baby cards.) About what percentage of the cards reflect the groups mentioned above? Check cards for stereotypic "humor" which exploits women and minorities, such as Native Americans and Asians.

- If you are dissatisfied with your findings, share your feelings with the clerk or buyer. Offer suggestions for improving the card selection. What else can you do?

3. Food Stores

➤ Check stores for employment percentages. Estimate how many people are working during your visit. How many are people of color? Manager? Checkers? Butchers? Produce workers? Baggers? Do these figures adequately reflect the diversity of the community? What percentage of the customers are people of color? Is there a contradiction?

- Question why more people of color are not employed at this store. What else can you do?

4. Banks

➤ Observe bank employment patterns. About how many persons are working at a given time? How many of these employees are people of color? In what capacity? What conclusion can you draw? Do the figures adequately reflect the diversity of the community?

- Inquire whether there are people of color working in the loan department, in top management, or on the board of directors. What can you do with this information?

5. Baby Products

➤ Check all baby product labels at the food store for images. What percentage of pictures on baby products are white? Compare your findings with baby products sold in the infant department of a department store or discount store.

- Write a letter to any of the manufacturers and inquire about their packaging practices. What else can you do?

6. Magazines and Newspapers at Major Food Stores or Drugstores

➤ Are copies of African American magazines and publications from other groups of color available? If newspapers are sold, are copies of any of the African American newspapers available? How about newspapers of any group of color? Of the available magazines, make a rough count and note how many display a person of color on the cover.

- Request that the store have magazines and newspapers from communities of color available for their customers. What else you can do?

7. Children's Toy Catalogs

➤ Examine the various dolls in toy catalogs. If African American dolls are available, do they have authentic African features or do they retain white features? Note other toys and games. Are there images of people of color?

- Ask the overall question: What do children learn about people from the toys available in this catalog? What can you do to address this issue?

8. Bookstores

➤ Visit a bookstore and note the children's book section. Of the total number of children's books displayed, what is the approximate percentage of books dealing with African Americans? Native Americans? Hispanics? Asians? Are there any books displayed about heroes from those groups? Note: The same kind of study could be done in the children's section of your community's library.

- If you are dissatisfied with your findings, you might talk to the salesperson or librarian and explain why. What else can you do?

9. Food Products

➤ Note the packaging on food products in your home. Are there any people of color pictured on these packages? Do these images reflect stereotypes?

- If you discover stereotyped portrayals on food packages, write to the manufacturer and express your concern. What else can you do?

PRAYER SERVICE ON RESPONDING TO THE SIN OF RACISM

Call to prayer

Thank you, God of Justice and Hope, for gathering us in the presence of your Spirit of Love and for sending us Jesus as our model of inclusion. Open our minds and hearts as we confess our sinfulness and seek your mercy, as we listen to your Word and seek your courage. This we ask in the name of your Son Jesus. Let all of God's people say:

Response:

Amen.

Confession

Listen and respond to these words from our bishops:

Racism is a sin: a sin that divides the human family, blots out the image of God among specific members of that family, and violates the fundamental human dignity of those called to be children of the same Father. Racism is the sin that says some human beings are inherently superior and others essentially inferior because of race (Brothers and Sisters to Us).

Response:

Creator God, we ask forgiveness for the times we have not been your "beloved community"; for the times when we have asserted a sense of superiority or accepted in silence a sense of inferiority, because of race.

All too often the Church in our country has been for many a "white Church," a racist institution. . . . Each of us as Catholics must acknowledge a share in the mistakes and sins of the past. Many of us have been prisoners of fear and prejudice. We have preached the Gospel while closing our eyes to the racism it condemns. We have allowed conformity to social pressures to replace compliance with social justice (Brothers and Sisters to Us, #31–32).

Response:

We ask forgiveness for the times we have allowed conformity to social pressures or fear of what others might think or say to keep us from acting for racial justice.

Listen to the Word of God

As a body is one though it has many parts, and all the parts of the body, though many, are one body, so also Christ. For in one Spirit we were all baptized into one body, whether Jews or Greeks, slaves or free persons, and we were all given to drink of one Spirit (1 Corinthians 12:12–13).

Response:

We pray your own words Jesus—"May we all be one."

Litany

Let us listen and respond to Martin Luther King, Jr.'s final Christmas sermon, preached at Ebenezer Baptist Church, Atlanta, December 24, 1967.
Litany Based on Dr. King's "I Still Have a Dream" Sermon.

Reader:

"I tried to talk to the nation about a dream that I had. But I must confess to you today that not long after talking about that dream I started seeing it turn into a nightmare. Yes, I am personally the victim of deferred dreams, of blasted hopes. . . ."

Response:

We understand. Some of our own dreams have been deferred. And clearly, racism has not gone away.

Reader:

"But in spite of that, I close today by saying that I still have a dream. Because you know that you can't give up in life. If you lose hope, somehow you lose that vitality that keeps life moving. You lose that courage to be, that quality that helps you go on in spite of. . . ."

Response:

There have been times when we lost hope and gave up. But we ask you, Jesus, for the courage to keep on going, to keep our hope alive.

Reader:

"So this is our faith as we continue to hope—that if there is to be peace on earth and goodwill toward all, let us know that in the process we have cosmic companionship."

Response:

We pray that our faith and hope will be deepened. And help us, ever-present God, to sense your companionship as we go on.

Reader:

"So today I still have a dream—that we will rise up and come to see that we are made to live together as brothers and sisters."

Response:

Help us, Holy Spirit, to reach out across our racial and cultural differences and work to make this dream come true.

Reader:

"I still have a dream this morning—that one day every person of color in the world will be judged on the basis of the content of their character rather than the color of their skin; that everyone will respect the dignity and worth of human personality; and that brotherhood will be more than a few words at the end of a prayer, but the first order of business on every legislative agenda."

Response:

We ask you, Jesus, to help us stop judging people by the color of their skin. As we pray for an end to racism, we ask your help in challenging our political leaders to address racism more boldly.

Reader:

"I still have a dream today—that justice will roll down like water and righteousness like a mighty stream. . . . I still have a dream."

Response:

We ask you, Spirit of God, to give us the wisdom and courage to join others in turning the work for racial justice into a mighty stream.

Other Resources for Chapter 6 Activities

Listed below are some engaging stories for youth about racism as experienced by different groups of people of color. They are presented with activities in *Celebrating Racial Diversity* by Kathleen McGinnis.

- *Hoops*, by Walter Dean Myers. It's a basketball story, but even more it's a story of courage and compassion in the face of racial and economic injustice. See also books by the author on Malcolm X, Muhammad Ali, Amistad, and many more.

- *Winners*, by Mary-Ellen Lang Collura. A Native American youth struggles with his identity in a society full of misunderstanding and bigotry.

- *Rising Voices: Writings of Young Native Americans*, by Arlene Hirschfelder and Beverly R. Singer. Prose and poetry about issues of identity, family, education, culture, and harsh realities.

- *The Journey: Japanese Americans, Racism, and Renewal*, paintings and text by Sheila Hamanaka. The story of the internment of Japanese Americans during World War II.

Biographies, autobiographies, and videos of racial justice heroes like César Chávez, Rosa Parks, Malcolm X, Martin Luther King, Jr., Wilma Mankiller, Fannie Lou Hamer, and Maya Angelou reveal not only the realities of racism but also how to confront them. These videos include:

- *Eyes on the Prize* (PBS series of the civil rights movement)

- *Selma, Lord, Selma* (on the Selma civil rights marches in the 1960s)

- *Malcolm X* (Spike Lee's gripping account of the life of Malcolm X)

- *Four Little Girls* (on the bombing of a Birmingham, Alabama church killing four girls)

- *Mississippi Burning* (the 1988 story of the FBI investigation of the murder of four civil rights workers)

- *Ghosts of Mississippi* (the 1996 story of delayed justice in the murder of Medgar Evers)

- *The Long Walk Home* (fictional account of the Montgomery bus boycott)

- *Crash* (2005 fictional story of the complexities of racism and prejudice in Los Angeles)

- *A Soldier's Story* (the 1984 story of racism in the U.S. military)

- *Ruby Bridges* (the 1998 TV film on Ruby's incredible courage in integrating the New Orleans public schools)

- *The Rosa Parks Story* (2002 film story of the "mother of the civil rights movement")

The civil rights museums in Atlanta, Memphis, and Birmingham are moving places to visit as well as important sources of resources.

www.thekingcenter.org—the Martin Luther King, Jr., Center in Atlanta, Georgia
www.civilrightsmuseum.org—the National Civil Rights Museum in Memphis, Tennessee
www.bcri.org—the Civil Rights Institute in Birmingham, Alabama

Chapter 7

Justice and Poverty

(See pages 145–171 of *Catholic Social Teaching*)

Poverty has many faces: the "poverty of soul" which refers to a lack of meaning one faces in life because of an obsession for material goods; the "poverty of spirit" in which a person remains totally dependent on God; and "material poverty" in which even a person's basic physical needs are not met. The focus of this chapter is primarily on material poverty.

Chapter 7, Activity 1

The Realities of Poverty

Step 1—Introduction

This activity is designed to help students get beyond impersonal statistics, to encounter those who are the victims of poverty, to unlearn some of the myths about poverty and the poor, and to become more empathetic and courageous. The stories of Jenny Boyce and Trevor Ferrell help youth see that this kind of compassion and courage is not just for adults—the Student Text uses Dorothy Day as the example. The two stories balance each other, one local and one global, and illustrate the need to address poverty both at home and overseas. Both of these stories can also be used in activity 3 on the "Preferential Option for the Poor."

Step 2—Make the data on poverty more real

Reflection on the text

Have students read the items in "Evidence of Material Poverty" (pages 148–149 of the Student Text) and mark those items that touch or trouble them in some way, perhaps sharing these in groups of two or three. Ask which item(s) troubled them the most. Be sure to focus some time on the item about 40,000 children dying each day from starvation or hunger-related diseases. *Note:* This data can be updated through the websites listed at the end of the chapter (page 170 of the Student Text).

Focus on children

The Children's Defense Fund has a creative way of making the statistics on poverty in the United States more understandable and compelling. Go to their website—www.childrens defense.org—and click on "Data" and then click on each of these three measures:

- "Moments in America" (breaks down poverty facts minute by minute)

- "Each Day in America" (breaks down yearly data to a single day)

- "Where America Stands" (compares U.S. data with other industrialized nations)

Ask students to identify those data that really surprised or troubled them. Invite them to share what they learned with their family and/or other friends.

Step 3—Calculating the costs of poverty

Note: The "Planning a Budget" activity on page 213 in the Student Text could be used here for the minimum wage calculations.

Calculating the cost

Ask students to calculate how much income a full-time job at the minimum wage would generate. Find out from a nursing home what the current hourly pay is for their Certified Nursing Assistants and have students figure out how far this money would go each month to cover just the basics of food, rent, transportation, utilities, clothing, health care. Working with the "poverty line" according to Federal Poverty Guidelines or with the poverty lines in your state, try to create a budget. For instance, in Missouri in 2006, a single mother with two children loses Medicaid coverage if she makes more than $91 per week ($364 per month).

Discussion

Ask students to discuss what her options are when she or her children get sick.

- What would they do in her situation?

- What is the impact of poverty on the poor?

- What is the impact of poverty on their community and the nation as a whole?

Experience. What does poverty cost in terms of time?

Have students chart the situation of a working single mother without a car and a sick child. Identify in your community a neighborhood where they might live, where the child goes to school, where the nearest clinic is located, and where a possible place of employment (e.g., a nursing home or restaurant) would be located. Calculate the routes she would have to take on public transportation to get from work to school to the clinic and back home and how long this might take. Invite the students to travel this route on public transportation, determine the time it takes, and write out their feelings and thoughts after the experience. If helpful, use the handout "Reflection on Personal Experiences" (page 126).

Step 4—Meeting and listening to the poor

Music for this step

Several songs from the album *J-Walking*, by Bryan Sirchio, are especially appropriate for this step. The first two songs focus on the theme as a whole, while the second two focus on Haiti and the experience of Jenny Boyce.

- "The Wooden Bell"—"no one listens to the cry of the poor."

- "Westbound on I-80"—a father encounters a homeless person without shoes and returns to give him his own.

- "Sarah's Song"—how a week with an orphan in Haiti completely changed this youth.

- "If You Eat Each Day"—a poor Haitian confronts a U.S. visitor about his wealth.

Reflection on the story of Jenny Boyce

Distribute the student handout "Jenny Boyce, A Teen Whose Life Was Changed" (pages 123–124). Have students read her story and write their answers to the questions that follow. Discuss especially what she learned from the poor and how this experience touched and changed her life.

Class speaker(s)

An easy way to hear from the poor about what it's like to be poor would be to invite one or several persons, from a shelter, church, or other agency you know, to speak about his or her life.

Site visits

One step closer to understanding what it's like to be poor would be to visit, as a whole class or in smaller groups, one of the shelters or agencies where the students are doing service projects. It would be best if several persons at the site could share their experiences of being poor, so that students can get a sense of the wide variety of backgrounds and life experiences that have placed people in poverty.

Individual encounters

If time permits, share the story of Trevor Ferrell and how his life changed because of his personal encounters with homeless people on the streets of Philadelphia. A high school junior in Kansas City, Missouri, shared her story of stopping to talk with a man holding a "Will work for food" sign and learned that he was an unemployed scientist. They talked for thirty minutes.

Encourage students to consider trying to meet and talk with someone poor with at least one classmate. There are definitely some risks involved, but it is also an opportunity to go way outside one's comfort zone and be touched more deeply than in a group visit. Some possibilities include:

- Arrange ahead of time to meet someone at a shelter, church, or other agency and invite this person to share some of their story with you.

- Stop and talk with someone holding a "Will work for food" sign.

- Find someone on a bus who has a long ride and ask if he or she would be willing to talk with you.

Students may find it helpful to arrange for a follow-up conversation, which could develop into a mutually beneficial relationship.

Step 5—Reflection and sharing

Written reflection

Distribute the handout "Reflection on Personal Experiences" (page 126) and answer any questions about what the handout is asking students. If time permits and all the categories are appropriate, invite students to write their thoughts and feelings about their experience(s). If time is limited, ask them to address the four final questions.

- What was the most memorable part of the whole experience?

- What did you learn about poverty and the poor through the experience(s)?

- What did you learn about yourself?

- What did you learn about God and your faith?

Sharing their reflections

Invite students to share their reflections in groups of two or three. Also invite them to share them more broadly—with family and friends, in a letter to the school or local newspaper, in a letter to their political representatives, and to the person(s) whose story they learned.

Jenny Boyce, A Teen Whose Life Was Changed

The plane soars over dusty brown mountains, and we descend for the landing. My mind races, wondering what will be in store for me in this desolate country of Haiti, the poorest in the Western Hemisphere. A Haitian's life expectancy is forty-seven, mine is seventy-two. Why did I first go to Haiti five years ago? I was a high school sophomore and went to see a slide show by two seniors who had just returned from two weeks in Haiti for their senior project. They showed slides of children so malnourished that they could not move, of slums unimaginably poor. But also in these slides I saw love, huge smiles, and lots of giving. In Rachel and Jennifer's voices I heard love, caring, and excitement about what they had experienced. I went home and told my family about it. Mom and Dad said it sounded like quite an experience, but wasn't sixteen too young to experience such poverty and difference in culture? Before we could discuss it further, Haiti had a violent revolution, so going was almost out of the question. As the year progressed, however, things in Haiti quieted down and we discussed it further and the rest of my family decided to join me. On December 27, 1986, the four of us were on the plane to Haiti!

In 1991 we took our fifth trip to Haiti as part of the Haiti Project of People-to-People in St. Louis. In these five years, I have encountered many people that have changed my life and values dramatically. At the boys orphanage, we lived the same life as the boys did, giving a wonderful feeling of being close to the culture and people. The boys live a very simple life with very few belongings or "conveniences," which leaves room for lots of love and growth in life. This is an important lesson I learned from them and I try to imitate it in everyday life. I have found that people who rely on material goods for happiness can never be satisfied because there are always more "things" to acquire, and many times many of these things are financially out of reach. But by valuing people, we always have a vast supply of happiness available.

My second year I decided to give Sans Fil, the home for dying adults, a try. The first day I was very quiet. I felt more comfortable with the women and did little things like giving lotion rubs for their dry skin and watching their faces light up when I painted their nails. I thought it would be very depressing, but they were so full of strength and pride that I left with a great amount of emotion. I came back day after day and got to know the women well. I was feeding the sickest ones by the end of the week and singing songs with some of the healthier ones. I had also ventured down to the men's quarters and was feeding them and giving them lotion rubs too. Last year I bandaged some of the sickest wounds I have ever seen, so bad that I was the one crying while I cleaned them. I feel that when I bandage wounds, I am actually giving these people tangible, physical help. The emotional support that we give by just talking to them, laughing with them, and massaging their dry, worn-out shoulders, helps them to feel human. It also helps them to die with some dignity and love, for lots of these people are found dying on the streets, with no one in the world to help them.

The smiles and comfort I have given to these people is extremely minute compared to what they have given me. . . . There is one woman in particular that I worked with. Her name is Marie (see my picture of us here), and in the short time that I knew her, she taught me endurance, patience, pride, and compassion. She had a large tumor removed from her eye. The result was a huge cavity that took up half of her face and was at least two inches deep in places. She knew she was going to die soon, but instead of wallowing in her pain and grief, she would try to talk to me and smile when I painted

her nails. We would sing together, since music is an easy way to communicate. I never once heard her complain. When I had to clean her wound, I would cry to see how much pain she must have been in. The amazing thing was that when I cried, she would comfort me, telling me not to worry, to keep working, all the while shaking with pain. I have a life that, in some ways, is hundreds of times better and yet I don't value my life nearly as much as she did. I whine and baby myself when I have a tiny case of the flu, and I know that I'm going to get better! Life looks completely different after my short encounter with this wonderful human being. I now try not to complain when I am uncomfortable or ill. I push myself more and challenge my endurance, each time learning and growing and loving life all the more. The most valuable lesson that I have learned from Marie is the value of human life. Since knowing her, I want to live life to the fullest and help others to do so too. . . .

I have come to realize that I cannot continue to live apathetically or materialistically after seeing the way that other people live. So I began to change the way I live, like conserving waste and energy, buying used clothes, emphasizing people instead of things in my life. . . . I work in a soup kitchen once a week and help Habitat for Humanity build houses for low income families in my community. . . . When I look back, it is hard to believe that a slide show could change my life this much!

➤ *What touched you the most about Jenny's story? Why?*

➤ *What did Jenny learn about people who are poor? What did they teach her?*

➤ *How did Jenny's life change because of these experiences?*

➤ *What helped Jenny overcome her feelings of being uncomfortable, even disgusted, at some of the poverty and disease she saw? Do you ever have similar feelings when you are around hurting people?*

➤ *What led Jenny to do what she did? Are there similar invitations in your life to "get involved"? How?*

THE STORY OF TREVOR FERRELL

At age eleven, Trevor saw a TV news clip about the homeless in Philadelphia and talked his father into driving him through areas where the homeless hang out. During this trip, Trevor jumped out of the car and gave a pillow and a blanket to a man sleeping on the streets. For six years after that night, December 8, 1983, Trevor did not miss a night on the streets! The following nights he took food and eventually "Trevor's Campaign" grew to feed hundreds of people nightly out of a traveling van. He mobilized other volunteers to open a temporary shelter for up to forty homeless men, women, and children and a thrift shop to collect donations and clothes. Within months, "Trevor's Campaign" had opened "Next Door," a shelter complete with a range of social services for health, employment, etc. During high school, Trevor twice visited and worked with Mother Teresa in Calcutta. After high school, Trevor continued to stay in touch with people on the streets and nurture some special friendships in his shelter. Occasionally he gave speeches on the importance of such work, even though this did not come easy to this shy and unassuming young man.

What Trevor has said, and what others have said about Trevor:

"I am only one, but still I am one.

I cannot do everything,

but still I can do something.

But because I can't do everything,

I will not refuse to do something I can do."

"The parable of the Good Samaritan certainly applies to Trevor. Philadelphia, 'the City of Brotherly Love,' is enhanced because of him, and so is our nation as a whole!"
—President Ronald Reagan, March 14, 1984

"I consider Trevor a soul mate. I am an adult fighting to aid children and he is a child fighting to aid adults. Trevor is the best example of compassion my daughter, Samantha, will ever have."
—Sally Struthers, actress

"When taunted by his classmates—'Hey, Trevor, got a blanket for me?'—Trevor replied, 'If I see you on 8th and Walnut, I'll be glad to give you one.' Some boys had hit him at recess in the school yard, and he was hurting on the inside too. He felt like an outsider. He never told us in those first months, but he would sometimes go quietly to his room and cry."
—Frank and Janet Ferrell, his parents, in *Trevor's Place*, Ferrell Family Endeavors, Inc., Gladwyne, PA, p. 19

"To the question 'what have you learned from helping street people?' Trevor replied: 'It's taught me that people aren't always what they seem to be. They might look mean to you, but when you go over to them, they're good, they're nice.'"
—*Trevor's Place*, p. 106

➤ *How did Trevor's life change because of his encounters with homeless people?*

➤ *What feelings does Trevor's story stir up in you?*

➤ *How can you respond to his challenge?*

REFLECTION ON PERSONAL EXPERIENCES

Observations—"During this experience I observed . . ."

➤ *I saw . . .*

➤ *I heard . . .*

➤ *I smelled . . .*

➤ *I touched . . .*

➤ *I tasted . . .*

Feelings—"When I made these observations, I felt . . ."

➤ *If sad, why?*

➤ *If angry, why?*

➤ *If afraid, why?*

➤ *If joyful, why?*

➤ *If ashamed, why?*

➤ *Other feelings and why . . .*

Desires and needs

➤ *"After this experience, I want to . . ."*

➤ *"In the future, I will . . ."*

➤ *"I feel grateful for . . ."*

➤ *"In this situation, God's help is needed to . . ."*

Key concluding questions

➤ *What was the most memorable part of the whole experience?*

➤ *What did you learn about poverty and the poor through the experience(s)?*

➤ *What did you learn about yourself?*

➤ *What did you learn about God and your faith?*

Chapter 7, Activity 2

Countering Consumerism

Step 1—Introduction

This activity is designed to challenge students to put Scripture and Church teaching into practice, especially in terms of their personal lifestyle. The two websites in step 4 are especially helpful and should be reviewed before using this activity. You will find many other suggestions for engaging students on this challenging issue.

Depending on the length of your sessions, this activity might best be done in two periods, with steps 2 and 3 for the first period and step 4 for the second period.

Step 2—Scripture and Church teaching

Reflection on the Scriptures

Choose those Scriptural passages in the Student Text, pages 151-153, that you especially want to focus on. Read them prayerfully and invite student reflection. Use the questions with the passages under "Scripture Link" for discussion.

Reflection on the Church Fathers

Have students read the passage from Saint John Chrysostom on page 160 of the Student Text; and then read this passage from Pope Paul VI quoting Saint Ambrose:

To quote Saint Ambrose: "You are not making a gift of your possessions to the poor. You are handing over to him what is his. . . . No one is justified in keeping for their exclusive use what they do not need, when others lack necessities." (Pope Paul VI, Development of Peoples, #23).

Ask the students what is meant by the quotations "the goods we possess are not ours, but theirs" and that we may be "stealing from them."

Step 3—Contemporary prophetic voices challenging U.S. consumerism

Reflection on Martin Luther King, Jr

Distribute the handout "Prophetic Voices Challenge U.S. Consumerism/Materialism" (page 130) and have students read aloud together the passage from Martin Luther King, Jr. Discuss the first two questions as a whole class. Invite students to write their answers to the last two questions in silence, perhaps sharing in groups of two or three one thing they wrote.

Reflection on the Catholic Bishops of Appalachia

Have students read aloud together the passage from the pastoral letter on Appalachia. Discuss the first five questions with the group. For the last question, ask the students to write their individual answers before sharing with a partner or small group.

Step 4—Suggestions and decisions on challenging consumerism

Background

This step picks up from the final question of step 3 and focuses on how to resist the attacks of consumerism.

Discussion

Distribute the student handout "Personal Decisions for Countering Consumerism" (page 131). Focus first on the subtitle—"Live more simply, so others can simply live"—and discuss with students the relationship between some people living in wealth and most people living in poverty. In what ways could one be the cause of the other? How could our living more simply enable the poor to simply live?

Reflection

Ask students to read over the list of practical suggestions and mark those that they are already doing or could see themselves doing. Ask them to write a plan for the future.

Discussion

Go through the list aloud, item by item, and identify what students are doing or could be doing for each. Encourage them to write some new ideas they hear from their classmates. List on newsprint or the board the various answers students wrote to the "What else could you do?" question, and encourage them to write new ideas that appeal to them.

Further research

Either in class or before the next class, have students visit two very helpful and creative web-sites for youth on this issue, find additional suggestions for action, and bring these back to class for group consideration.

Affluenza: www.pbs.org/kcts/affluenza

The Center for a New American Dream: www.newdream.org

Decisions

Read aloud the three suggestions for making decisions and getting started and discuss any questions these raise. Encourage the students to identify someone who could support them in their efforts to change (#2). Then invite them to choose one of the suggestions to start with, circle it, and decide when and how they will begin to put it into practice.

Note: A possible addition to the initial discussion in step 4—on the connection between wealthy lifestyles for a few and poverty for many: Share with students the visual on the "Survival of the Fattest" (from *Bread and Justice: Toward a New International Economic Order*, by James McGinnis, Paulist Press, 1979, p. 307).

Observe that as obesity becomes a greater and greater issue in the United States, hunger continues to flourish in this country and overseas. Is there a connection between the two? Is there a suggestion for action in this?

PROPHETIC VOICES CHALLENGE U.S. CONSUMERISM/MATERIALISM

Martin Luther King, Jr.

". . . We as a nation must undergo a radical revolution of values. We must rapidly begin the shift from a thing-oriented society to a person-oriented society. When machines and computers, profit motives and property rights, are considered more important than people, the giant triplets of racism, extreme materialism, and militarism are incapable of being conquered" (from "When Silence Is Betrayal," April 4, 1967).

1. In what ways is our society "thing-oriented"?

2. Do you agree with King that "machines and computers, profit motives and property rights, are considered more important than people"? Why or why not?

3. How "thing-oriented" are you?

4. How could you become less "thing-oriented" and more "person-oriented"?

Catholic Bishops of Appalachia

"Many times before, outside forces have attacked the mountain's dream. But never before was the attack so strong. Now it comes with cable TV, satellite communications, giant ribbons of highway driving into the guts of the land. The attack wants to teach people that happiness is what you buy—in soaps and drinks, in gimmicks and gadgets, and that all of life is one big commodity market. It would be bad enough if the attack only tried to take the land, but it wants the soul too" (*This Land Is Home to Me*, 1974).

1. Who or what are these "outside forces"?

2. What do they mean by "happiness is what you buy . . ." and "all of life is one big commodity market"?

3. Name the different places where you hear this message.

4. Consider these facts and questions:

> *• 93 percent of teen-aged girls say store-hopping is their favorite activity.*
>
> *• Before they graduate from high school, typical American students have been exposed to 360,000 ads; 30,000 of those before they entered first grade.*
>
> *• What is your reaction to these statistics? If you have no reaction, why do you think that is so?*

5. How is this mentality an "attack on the soul"?

6. How has it attacked your own soul?

PERSONAL DECISIONS FOR COUNTERING CONSUMERISM

"Live more simply, so others can simply live."

Some practical ways to counter consumerism

Use public facilities

➤ Use the public library for books and videos and public parks for outdoor fun.

Critique advertising

➤ As a way of resisting the appeal of advertising, talk back to TV commercials, magazine ads, highway billboards. Share some of this with your friends or family.

Enjoy the outdoors

➤ The beauty of creation can delight more than the latest technology. Walk or bike in nearby parks. Try hiking and canoeing, or an overnight campout. Enjoy your local botanical gardens and arboretums and visit state and national parks whenever you get the opportunity.

Think before you buy

➤ Are you an impulsive buyer or affected by the push to instant gratification? Is there a way you could slow down your shopping habits to allow for some time to reflect about whether you need an item before you purchase it?

Personalize your gifts

➤ Personal "presence" can be more satisfying than purchased presents when we celebrate birthdays, holidays, and other special occasions. Surprise parties, albums with special photos and personal statements, homemade gifts, and going to special places with the person being celebrated are all wonderful alternatives to consumer-oriented rituals.

Shop small

➤ Shop at local stores and thrift stores, buy from local producers (e.g., open air or farmers markets), and eat at neighborhood restaurants.

Consider the mall and other "superstores" (e.g. Wal-Mart, Circuit City, Best Buy)

➤ *Malls and superstores are everywhere, replacing many local stores and family-owned restaurants. How often and for what reasons do you shop or eat at large chains?*

➤ *What functions have the shopping mall and superstores taken on in our nation? In your own life?*

➤ *True or false: shopping malls and superstores have become the religious temples of America. Explain.*

Institute an "Exchange System"

➤ *To reduce the amount of "stuff" you accumulate, for each new item you buy, give away a similar item to someone in need. This works especially well with articles of clothes but can also apply to books, games, CDs, DVDs, etc.*

What else could you do?

Three suggestions as you make your decisions and start putting them into practice

1. *You don't have to do everything right away, but you should do something. As you get used to simplifying in one area, you can consider other changes. (It's a journey.)*

2. *Look for others who can support you—family members, friends, other peers or adults in school, in your neighborhood, faith community, or wider community. Change is easier, and more enjoyable, when done with others.*

3. *Make changes that bring you joy. They won't always be easy, but they should give you a deep sense of satisfaction.*

Chapter 7, Activity 3

Preferential Option for the Poor

Step 1—Introduction

The segment of the Student Text on "A Christian Response to Poverty: Preferential Option for the Poor" (pages 160–162) is critically important. It challenges us to go far beyond donating money or serving at a soup kitchen. It challenges us to make the poor a real priority in our lives—a "preferential option" for our time, talent, and treasure. Ultimately, the Church is asking us to embrace those who are poor with the same love that God has for them.

In *Faces of Poverty, Faces of Christ* (Orbis Books, 1991), Mev Puleo's photographs of the poor, as well as John Kavanaugh's text on poverty, make a compelling combination and ideal book for this activity and unit as a whole. Fritz Eichenberg's images of Christ and the poor are classic, especially the Last Supper of Jesus and the poor.

The films of Gerard Thomas Straub are even more compelling for putting faces on the poor and inviting students to see in them the face of Christ. In *Poverty and Prayer*, this ex-Hollywood soap opera producer and now deeply compassionate and committed Catholic filmmaker presents ten- to thirty-minute excerpts from five of his films. It begins with a two-minute introduction putting the text of Matthew 25:31–46 behind riveting images of the faces of the poor. See "Other Resources for Chapter 7 Activities," pages 139–140, for more ideas.

The following six of the songs on *J-Walking*, by Bryan Sirchio, are helpful for this whole activity, with the first two especially appropriate for step 2:

- "Yesterday I Saw Jesus"—on encountering Jesus in the outcasts and poor.

- "I See You"—really noticing the invisible poor and searching for helpful responses.

- "Sarah's Song"—how a week with an orphan in Haiti completely changed this youth.

- "The Wooden Bell"—"no one listens to the cry of the poor."

- "Westbound on I-80"—a father encounters a homeless person without shoes and returns to give him his own.

- "If You Eat Each Day"—a poor Haitian confronts a U.S. visitor about his wealth.

Step 2—The faces of "the least" brothers and sisters of Jesus

Reflection on Matthew 25:31–46

How clear this priority of reaching out to our "least" brothers and sisters is revealed in Scripture passages in the Student Text, pages 151–153. Read and discuss these as time permits. Focus especially on Matthew 25:31–46 and what Jesus means by "insofar as you did this to one of the least of these, you did it to me." Consider using an excerpt from *Poverty and Prayer* as a way of combining the text and the faces.

Focus on the faces

Ask students if they can recall the face of any poor person they noticed in the past week—either in person or in the news—and what they noticed about that face. Very few students will probably recall any faces. Ask what that says to them. Then ask students to look briefly at the faces of the people on pages 145, 148, 154, and 156 in their text and then choose that face that most draws their attention. Ask them to focus on that one face for several minutes and try to see Jesus in that person's face. Then ask them to think about how much God must love that person and invite them to write these thoughts in prose or as a prayer in a journal or on a separate sheet of paper.

Discussion

Explore with the students why it is that so often the poor are invisible to middle- and upper-middle-class people, why they so seldom really see the faces of the poor.

Step 3—The witness of others

Discussion

Share and discuss one or more of the following witnesses of what it ultimately means to make a "preferential option for the poor," as Jesus did. Dorothy Day is discussed in their text, pages 166–167, and the quotation from Jean Donovan is on the student handout. For students who have a hard time understanding what "preferential option" really means, you might equate it with "being in love." As Archbishop Romero puts it below, "I give my life for those whom I love. . . ."

Dorothy Day

For more on Dorothy Day, see "Other Resources for Chapter 7 Activities," page 139.

Jean Donovan

Martyred in 1980 because of her work with the poor in El Salvador, this young lay woman had been tempted to leave the country because of the pleas of her fiancé and family. "Several times I have decided to leave El Salvador. I almost could except for the children, the poor, bruised victims of this insanity. Who would care for them? Whose heart could be so staunch as to favor the reasonable thing in a sea of their tears and loneliness? Not mine, dear friend, not mine" (*Salvador Witness* by Ana Carrigan, p. 212).

Archbishop Romero

The Paulist Productions film *Romero* is the most compelling version of Romero's story for youth. You might use the following quotation as a short way of introducing Archbishop Romero:

> It took a lifetime for Archbishop Romero to make his preferential option for the poor. Most of his life was spent in academia and in the circles of the wealthy of El Salvador. It wasn't until after he was made the Archbishop of San Salvador that he made his option for the poor. But when he did, it was total.

> "I rejoice, brothers and sisters, that our church is persecuted precisely for its preferential option for the poor, and for seeking to become incarnate in the interests of the poor . . . . The Church suffers the lot of the poor: persecution . . ." (February 17, 1980).

> "As a pastor I am bound by a divine command to give my life for those whom I love, and that includes all Salvadorans, even those who are going to kill me" (March 10, 1980).

Step 4—Making a preferential option for the poor

Background

Most people are not called to do what Dorothy Day, Archbishop Romero, and Jean Donovan did. But we are called to move in the direction of their lives, for this is the path of Jesus. As his followers, we are called to embrace the least of his people and make them a priority for our time, talent, and treasure, and above all, a priority in our heart. Perhaps the most important item on the handout on "Making a Preferential Option for the Poor" is developing friendships with those who are economically poor. We are much more willing to sacrifice on behalf of people we know and care about.

As part of the reflection and discussion, be sure to integrate the "What Can You Do?" reflection in the Student Text, page 157. As part of the discussion of "A Solidarity Day," integrate "The Eucharist and the Hungry," page 159 of the Student Text, since the Eucharist is all about solidarity.

Reflection

Taking one category at a time, invite students to write their responses to each of the questions on the handout. It might be helpful to solicit some examples of doing each of the categories before asking students to answer the questions.

Discussion

Taking one category at a time, invite students to share their answers preferably with the whole group. List on newsprint or the board the suggestions they identify for the "What else could you do?" questions. See what questions emerge from answering the questions and discuss those that are the most pertinent. Be sure to discuss the suggestion of "A Solidarity Day."

Decisions

Invite students to answer the decision question at the bottom of the handout—"What is your next step in making a preferential option for the poor?" Then make a decision about a possible group observance of "A Solidarity Day."

MAKING A PREFERENTIAL OPTION FOR THE POOR

Making the poor a priority with your talents

➤ What have you already done to share your talents (as a tutor, mentor, musician, camp counselor, etc.) with poor children? With the elderly poor?

➤ What else could you do?

➤ As you think about possible careers, what would they enable you to do on behalf of the poor?

Making the poor a priority with your treasure

➤ In what ways are you using any of your money or possessions to benefit the poor?

➤ When you buy gifts, have you ever shopped at stores that feature the handicrafts of economically poor artisans? Research and name such a store in your area

➤ How often do you donate some of your clothing, books, DVDs, etc., to the poor and/or encourage others in your family to share their toys and other possessions?

➤ What else could you do?

Making the poor a priority with your time

➤ How can you make time to visit those who are poor, to learn about poverty and those who are working for economic justice? What kinds of service projects have you done with the poor?

➤ Do you write letters to your political representatives on behalf of the poor? What topic do you think you can write about?

➤ What else could you do?

Making the poor a priority in your hearts

➤ Here's what Jean Donovan, a young U.S. lay woman who was martyred because she worked with the poor, said about the priority of the El Salvadoran children in her heart: "Several times I have decided to leave El Salvador. I almost could except for the children, the poor, bruised victims of this insanity. Who would care for them? Whose heart could be so staunch as to favor the reasonable thing in a sea of their tears and loneliness? Not mine, dear friend, not mine."

➤ How can you develop a mutual friendship with someone who is poor?

➤ How often and how specifically do you pray for the poor and for the compassion and courage to reach out to the poor and work for economic justice?

➤ How can you stand up for the poor when others are making jokes or saying degrading things about the poor?

"A Solidarity Day"

➤ Would you be willing to commit one day a month to focus on the poor and make it a day of sacrificing some of your treasure, talent, and time on behalf of the poor? Pray especially on that day for the poor. Skip a meal and/or snacks and donate the savings.

Decision:

➤ What is your next step in making a preferential option for the poor?

Other Resources for Unit 7 Activities

For Activity 2 on Countering Consumerism

Alternatives for Simple Living (www.simpleliving.org) is a nonprofit organization helping people of faith challenge consumerism, live justly, and celebrate responsibly. Started in 1973 as a protest against the commercialization of Christmas, its focus is on encouraging celebrations that reflect conscientious ways of living. Their resources include:

- **Affluenza—The All-Consuming Epidemic**, a video showing how problems like loneliness and rising debt, longer working hours and environmental pollution, family conflict and rampant commercialism are actually symptoms of "affluenza," the never-ending search for more; plus many treatments that offer hope for recovery.

- **Break Forth Into Joy—Beyond a Consumer Lifestyle**, a video exploring consumerism and its effects on people and the earth; plus actions for individuals and families.

For Activity 3 on Preferential Option for the Poor

The films and witness of Gerard Thomas Straub After renouncing his Hollywood lifestyle by 1995, Gerard responded to God's call to find Jesus in the faces and lives of those who are poor and to share this challenging vision with youth and adults. Each of these five films is available on DVD and VHS for $30 from the San Damiano Foundation—www.SanDamianoFoundation.org; (818) 563-1947.

- **Poverty and Prayer**, a 90-minute film, presents ten- to thirty-minute excerpts from his five main films on seeing and responding to Christ in the poor. Each segment is sprinkled with his prayerful biblical commentary, but it is the faces and the beginnings of the stories of the poor that are so compelling. Each of these films is a photographic meditation on the plight of the poor, the presence of Jesus in the poor, and our responsibility to help.

- **When Did I See You Hungry?**, a 37-minute film narrated by Martin Sheen, features rare footage from inside a leprosarium in Brazil, plus 250 poignant black and white photographs from slums in nine nations, revealing the hidden humanity of the poor and their spirit of joy and will to survive.

- **Embracing the Leper**, a 32-minute film, tells the inspirational story of a secular Franciscan working with people with leprosy and extreme poverty. It's difficult both to look and not look at these rejected children of God.

- **Rescue Me**, a 200-minute film, reveals the horrific plight of the poor and homeless of Skid Row in downtown Los Angeles and the heroic work of the Union Rescue Mission. Since it is difficult to take in so many painful images for over three hours, the 30-minute excerpt from *Poverty and Prayer* may be more appropriate.

- **Endless Exodus**, a 130-minute film, portrays the sorrowful flight of desperate Central Americans whose options are "go North or go hungry," focusing particularly on one Salvadoran family with whom the filmmaker lived for a month.

- **The Sun and Moon Over Assisi,** (St. Anthony Messenger, 2000) is Gerard's own conversion story woven into his experiences of the lives and spirituality of Francis and Clare during his pilgrimages to Assisi.

On Dorothy Day

Jim Forest's biography, *Love Is the Measure* (Paulist Press, 1986), is perhaps the best. The Paulist Productions film *Entertaining Angels* focuses especially on Dorothy's early activism and her conversion to Jesus and his commitment to peace and compassion.

On Archbishop Romero

For books, his diary entitled *Archbishop Oscar Romero: A Shepherd's Diary* (St. Anthony Messenger Press, 1993), and Jon Sobrino's *Archbishop Romero: Memories and Reflections* (Orbis Books, 1990) are good background.

Chapter 8

Justice and Peace

(See pages 173–201 of *Catholic Social Teaching*)

All Christians are called to work for peace in the world. In order to achieve peace, Christians are called to cooperate with God's grace to create societies that work to attain the common good. Through the Youth Pledge of Nonviolence, this unit challenges youth to be peacemakers in their interpersonal relationships as well as in the global community.

Chapter 8, Activity 1

"Blessed Are the Peacemakers"

Step 1—Introduction

While "peace" and "peacemaking" are so central to the words and witness of Jesus, they tend to generate just the opposite in personal conversations as well as in public debate. Perhaps this is part of what Jesus meant when he said, "Do you think that I have come to establish peace on the earth? No, I tell you, but rather division . . . a father will be divided against his son and a son against his father . . ." (Luke 12:51–53). You might ask students to compare their own opinions on issues of war and peace with that of their parents.

But the Church is as clear as the Gospel that peacemaking is core to the Christian vocation. "Peacemaking is not an optional commitment. It is a requirement of our faith. We are called to be peacemakers, not by some movement of the moment, but by our Lord Jesus" (U.S. Catholic Bishops, *The Challenge of Peace*, 1983, #332).

In this first activity of this chapter, the focus will be on exploring Jesus' challenging way of peace. This activity will expand on several segments in the Student Text—"Spirituality of Peacemaking" (pages 176–177), "The Meaning of Peace in the Bible" (pages 179–180), and "Levels of Violence" (pages 181–182).

Step 2—God's "peace"

Word association

Ask the students to say aloud what words or phrases come immediately to mind when you say the word "peace." List these on newsprint or the board. Probably one of these phrases will be something like "absence of conflict." This would provide the opportunity to distinguish the terms "positive peace" and "negative peace," as Dr. King did in his "Letter From Birmingham Jail." A "negative peace" is one where order is maintained by force. More than once Dr. King heard the words, "We didn't have any problem until that troublemaker came to town." But a "negative peace" just hides problems which have to be brought to the surface and lanced, as one lances a boil, so that healing can begin. The outcome hopefully will be a "positive peace" where everyone's rights and needs are recognized and protected.

Input and discussion

Ask the students if they know God's word for peace in Hebrew ("Shalom") and then what it means. "Shalom" includes harmony, unity, justice, and prosperity—"positive peace." When Jeremiah says that the people cry out, "Shalom! Shalom!" but there is no Shalom (Jeremiah 6:13–15), he is precisely condemning the people for their lack of integrity and justice, without which "Shalom" is an empty word.

Prayerful reflection

Ask students to reflect in silence on Jesus' words in his Sermon on the Mount—"Blessed are the peacemakers, for they will be called the children of God" (Matthew 5:9).

Discussion

Ask students:

- What does Jesus mean by "peacemakers"? What do peacemakers do?

- Why are peacemakers especially blessed in Jesus' estimation?

- What is it about "peacemaking" that makes us "children of God"?

Step 3—Jesus' plea for peace

Background

Scripture records only three times when Jesus wept—over the death of his friend Lazarus, during his agony in the garden, and over Jerusalem before his entry into his beloved "city of peace," which is the meaning of the word "Jeru-salem."

Visual meditation

Read Jesus' words—"If only today you knew the things that make for peace" (Luke 19:42) and ask students to repeat these words several times. Then invite students to look into the face of the weeping Jesus (on the handout "Litany on the Nonviolence of Jesus, page 150") and think about what those tears are saying.

Discussion

Ask students:

- Why did Jesus weep over Jerusalem?

- What were some of the forms of violence about which Jesus was so upset that he wept? (You might use the components of the "Litany on the Nonviolence of Jesus, page 150," to supplement the students' responses.)

- What future did Jesus see for Jerusalem if the people didn't repent from their violent ways?

Read aloud the conclusion of this passage (Luke 19:43–44):

> ". . . But now it is hidden from your eyes. For the days are coming upon you when your enemies will raise a palisade against you; they will encircle you and hem you in on all sides. They will smash you to the ground and your children within you, and they will not leave one stone upon another within you because you did not recognize the time of your visitation."

Step 4—Applying this plea to our own time and place

Background

This visual of Jesus weeping is actually a statue of Jesus at the bombsite in Oklahoma City, where 168 persons were killed in April 1995. The Archdiocese of Oklahoma City erected the statue as a way of pleading for peace in our own time and place.

Visual meditation

Ask students to look at this statue opposite the bombsite (on the student handout "Litany on the Nonviolence of Jesus, page 150") and meditate on what Jesus might be weeping about in terms of the violence in our own society.

Discussion

Brainstorm with the students about all the different forms of violence in our own society that would make Jesus weep today. Use the "Levels of Violence" material (pages 181–182 of the Student Text) as a way of expanding on the forms of violence in our society.

Step 5—Jesus' way of peacemaking

a. The Donkey

Background

After weeping over Jerusalem because of its blindness to the things that make for peace, Jesus escalated his effort to show the way to peace. He climbed back on the donkey he had requested for his ride into Jerusalem at the very time that additional Roman soldiers were riding their stallions of war into the city to "keep the peace" during Passover. See the handout "On Being Jesus' 'Donkeys for Peace'" (page 149) for more background and for possible use with the students.

Scripture

Read Zechariah 9:9–10 to see why Jesus chose a donkey to dramatically demonstrate his way of peace:

> *Rejoice heartily, O daughter Zion, shout for joy, O daughter Jerusalem! See, your king shall come to you; a just savior is he, meek, and riding on an ass, on a colt, the foal of an ass. He shall banish the chariot from Ephraim, and the horse from Jerusalem; the warrior's bow shall be banished, and he shall proclaim peace to the nations.*

Discussion

Discuss the difference between donkeys and stallions. Many students probably remember the movie *Shrek 2*, where the donkey takes a magic potion to become a stallion. You might show the forty-second segment where the transformed donkey rejoices in its new identity. Ask:

- Why would donkeys rather be stallions?

- Which would you prefer to be, a donkey or a stallion, and why?

- Why do you think Jesus chose a donkey at the most critical moment in his ministry?

b. The Cross

Background

Within a week, Jesus' challenge to the lack of compassion, peace, and religious integrity (overthrowing the tables of the money-changers in the Temple and challenging the religious authorities) in Jerusalem leads him to the cross.

Visual meditation

Provide students with a crucifix to look at or use the image of the cross in the foreground of the exploding World Trade Center Towers on September 11, 2001 (available on the Institute for Peace and Justice website: www.ipj-ppj.org), and ask them to think about what the cross says about Jesus' way of peacemaking.

Discussion

Ask students for their reflections on the message of the cross and what it tells us about Jesus' response to violence and what it means to be a peacemaker.

c. "Some Biblical Seeds of Peace" (see page 148)

Background

This handout includes many of Jesus' teachings about his way of peacemaking, especially drawn from the Sermon on the Mount (Matthew 5:1–7:27) and the Sermon on the Plain (Luke 6:20–49). The title of the handout is drawn from the first passage—about the necessity of a seed to fall into the ground and die before it can bear fruit. The kernel of every seed of peace is the cross—the willingness of persons to die to themselves and focus on others, to risk themselves in showing compassion and challenging violence.

Silent reflection

Distribute the handout "Some Biblical Seeds of Peace" (page 148) and ask students to read the passages and reflect in writing on questions 1 and 2 at the bottom.

Discussion

Invite students to share their answers to questions 1 and 2 in groups of two or three. Focus on why some of the gospel passages are especially troubling or challenging.

Decisions

Ask students to pray over the passage they chose for question 2 and then write their answer to question 3. If time permits, invite them to share their answers to question 3 in the same small groups.

Checking back

In the next class, you might have students on how they carried out their decision in question 3.

Step 6—"On Being Jesus' 'Donkeys for Peace'"

If you want to further challenge the students to put Jesus' way of peace into practice, distribute the handout "On Being Jesus' 'Donkeys for Peace'" (page 149) and ask them to read it over prayerfully before the next class and answer the decision questions at the bottom of the page. Begin the next class by having the students report on their work.

Step 7—"Litany on the Nonviolence of Jesus"

Distribute the student handout "Litany on the Nonviolence of Jesus" (page 150) and pray it together as the conclusion of this activity.

SOME BIBLICAL SEEDS OF PEACE

"If a grain of wheat falls in the ground and dies, it yields a rich harvest" (John 12:24*).

"Love one another as I have loved you. . . . No greater love than to lay down your life" (John 15:12–13)

"By the blood of Christ we have been brought close together. He is the peace between us, breaking down barriers that used to keep us apart, . . . restoring peace through the cross" (Ephesians 2:13–16).

"Those who lose their lives for my sake and for the sake of the Gospel will find life" (Mark 8:35).

"Love your enemies; do good to those who persecute you" (Luke 6:27, 35; Matthew 5:44).

"Pray for those who persecute you; ask God to bless those who insult you" (Matthew 5:44; Luke 6:28).

"Seek first the Kingdom of God and then all these other things will be given you (Matthew 6:33).

"Forgive others and God will forgive you" (Luke 6:37).

"An eye for an eye? No, don't try to get even with those who have hurt you" (Matthew 5:38–39).

"Take the log out of your own eye . . ." (Luke 6:42).

"Turn the other cheek; walk the extra mile" (Luke 6:29; Matthew 5:40–42).

"Give to everyone who asks and . . . lend without expecting to be paid back" (Luke 6:30, 35).

"Blessed are the poor, the meek, the gentle . . ." (Matthew 5:3–4, 7).

"But woe to you rich and well-fed" (Luke 6:20–21, 24–25).

"Blessed are those who hunger and thirst for justice" (Matthew 5:6).

"Blessed are the peacemakers" (Matthew 5:9).

"Blessed are those who are persecuted in the cause of right" (Matthew 5:10).

"Integrity will bring peace; justice give lasting security" (Isaiah 32:17).

*Text in this passage has been abbreviated for emphasis.

Questions:

1. Which of these Scripture passages challenges you most at this moment?

2. Which most touches your heart and what does it reveal about the things that make for peace?

3. What one thing could you do specifically to put this passage into practice?

ON BEING JESUS' "DONKEYS FOR PEACE"

On Jesus' final journey into Jerusalem as an emissary of peace

As Jesus was coming down the Mount of Olives toward Jerusalem, he stopped at a vantage point where the whole of Jerusalem spread out before him. He gazed out at his "City of Peace," and wept. "Jerusalem, Jerusalem, if only today you knew the things that make for peace! But now it is hidden from your eyes. For the days are coming upon you when your enemies will raise a palisade against you; they will encircle you and hem you in on all sides. They will smash you to the ground and your children within you, and they will not leave one stone upon another within you because you did not recognize the time of your visitation" (Luke 19:41–44).

But this was not a "done deal." There was still time for Jerusalem to repent and embrace the things that make for peace. Jesus was determined to make his appeal one more time for God's inclusive community of love, love even for one's enemies. As a sign of his way of peace, he remounted his donkey and continued toward Jerusalem. Because this was the week of Passover and large crowds of Jews would be gathering in Jerusalem, the Romans were sending in armed reinforcements to "keep the peace." As the Roman military officers approached Jerusalem from one direction on their stallions of war, Jesus approached on his donkey of peace. Jesus knew the Scriptures and chose this symbol of nonviolent peacemaking to reinforce his message.

"Rejoice heartily, O daughter Zion, shout for joy, O daughter Jerusalem! See, your king shall come to you; a just savior is he, meek, and riding on an ass, on a colt, the foal of an ass. He shall banish the chariot from Ephraim, and the horse from Jerusalem; the warrior's bow shall be banished, and he shall proclaim peace to the nations" (Zechariah 9:9–10).

On the donkey as a symbol and instrument of peace

- Jesus rides a donkey into places of violence where peace is especially needed.

- The donkey enters the situation completely.

- Jesus isn't a warrior on a fast horse to ride in, inflict damage, and escape; but on a donkey he goes in to stay as long as it takes to work things out.

- The donkey runs the same risk of being killed as its rider.

On being Jesus' donkeys for peace

Jesus won't get to as many places or get there as fast if we and other donkeys aren't willing to be ridden into those situations. These situations could include:

- interpersonal situations—conflicts in our family, school, neighborhood, or workplace

- wider and deadlier conflicts—fights, riots, war zones

- institutional or social-political situations—in our Church, educational systems, government policies, corporate practices, the criminal justice system.

Personal decisions

➤ *Where do you think Jesus might be sending you at this moment as one of his "donkeys for peace"?*

➤ *What could you do in this situation to be his peacemaker?*

Litany on the Nonviolence of Jesus

Jesus, you wept over Jerusalem and its disregard of Samaritans and lepers, and you weep today over the escalating violence of racism and hate in our own society and world. Jesus, in the face of escalating violence,

Let us escalate love

Jesus, you wept over Jerusalem and its humiliating occupation by the Roman Empire, and you weep today over the escalating violence of terrorism in your Holy Land. Jesus, in the face of escalating violence,

Let us escalate love

Jesus, you wept over Jerusalem and its exploitation of the poor, and you weep today over the escalating violence of poverty in our own society and world. Jesus, in the face of escalating violence,

Let us escalate love

Jesus, you wept over Jerusalem and its disregard of women and children, and you weep today over escalating violence against women and children in our own society and world. Jesus, in the face of escalating violence,

Let us escalate love

Jesus, you wept over Jerusalem and its deadly use of weapons of violence, and you weep today over the proliferation of the weapons of violence, from handguns to nuclear bombs, in our own society and world. Jesus, in the face of escalating violence,

Let us escalate love

Jesus, you wept over Jerusalem where capital punishment was rampant, and you weep today over the escalating use of capital punishment in our own society. Jesus, in the face of escalating violence,

Let us escalate love

Jesus, you wept over Jerusalem where the forces of domination were everywhere, and you weep today over the escalating domination—all the "isms"—in our own society and world. Jesus, in the face of escalating violence,

Let us escalate love

Chapter 8, Activity 2

The Youth Pledge of Nonviolence

"In the Face of Escalating Violence, Escalate Love"

Step 1—Introduction

This activity tries to answer Jesus' plea to work and live for peace. Using the Youth Pledge of Nonviolence as one list or description of these peacemaking behaviors, it makes "The Option of Nonviolence" segment in the Student Text (pages 182–184) more specific, particularly in terms of interpersonal nonviolence or peacemaking.

The title of this activity is drawn from the "Litany on the Nonviolence of Jesus" (page 150). The phrase was the answer to a prayer in 1991, moments after the bombing of Iraq at the outbreak of the Gulf War. "Jesus, how do you want me to confront this new violence in our world?" This action-oriented mantra became embodied in the Pledge of Nonviolence five years later. The image of the scale with the two trays, one for the boulders of violence and the other for the pebbles of love illustrates the challenge to promote peace by escalating the works of love.

This activity could be used simply as the context for activity 3 on the forgiveness component of the Youth Pledge of Nonviolence. In that case, you could present just the background information in step 2. But this activity could be the focus of a full class or several classes. If you want to focus on the Youth Pledge for several classes, see the reflection pages on the other six components of the Pledge, plus other resources for living and teaching the Pledge, in Appendix A, pages 205–212.

Step 2—The Youth Pledge of Nonviolence

Background

This Youth Pledge was adapted from the Family Pledge of Nonviolence, which was formulated in 1996 by a coalition of faith communities, social service agencies, and other community groups convened by the Institute for Peace and Justice. It was part of a strategy for addressing the escalating violence in our society. The Pledge proclaims that peacemaking is more than occasional political action. It is a "24-7-365" way of living. The first four components of the Pledge focus on interpersonal peacemaking. The fifth component challenges us to create a more peaceful or harmonious relationship with the earth, which is the focus for Unit 10 of the Student Text. The sixth component challenges us to recreate and entertain ourselves in nonviolent ways, while the last component challenges us to confront the many other forms of violence in our society, some of which are treated in other units (e.g., Chapters 5–7 on prejudice, racism, and poverty). The violence of war will be examined in activity 3 to follow.

Student reflection

Distribute the "Youth Pledge of Nonviolence" (page 154), present some of the introductory and background information above, and ask students to read it over carefully as a description of those "things that make for peace." After pointing out that components 4 (forgiveness), 5 (respect nature), and 7 (courage) will be addressed in other activities, ask the students to choose one of the remaining four components as the one they would consider putting more into practice in their lives.

Small group brainstorming

Divide the class into groups according to which component of the Pledge each student chose. For groups with more than six students, break these into two smaller groups. Ask each group to identify as many different ways as they can for putting their specific component of the Pledge into practice.

Personal decisions

Ask each student to silently choose one of the ways discussed in their group to put their component of the Pledge into practice and write it on an index card. Invite members of each small group to share their decision aloud with the whole class. Encourage them to be specific.

Step 3—The boulders of violence and the pebbles of peace

Background

Given the enormity of the obstacles to peace, the small actions that we can take (like the decisions the students just made) often seem worthless. We need to stir the imaginations of students and plant a motivating vision that will increase the hope that our actions will make a difference. The scale balancing the boulders of violence with the pebbles of love helps provide this vision.

Discussion

Distribute the handout "Pebbles of Love Against the Boulders of Violence" (page 155). Read the first two paragraphs aloud together and ask students to identify other forms of violence that might be added to the tray of boulders. Then focus on the image and ask students which way they think the scale is tipping at this time in history. Read the "Confronting the Boulders" paragraph and ask students to name times when they have confronted any of the boulders of violence directly, and then indirectly.

Personal decisions

Ask students to read prayerfully "Being a 'Pebble of Love'" and then write their answer to the question below. This may be a reaffirmation of the decision they made earlier on putting their components of the Youth Pledge of Nonviolence into practice.

Step 4—"A Litany on the Pebbles of Love"

As a way of concluding this activity, pray together the "Litany on the Pebbles of Love" (page 156).

If possible, distribute to each student a pebble as a symbol of their willingness to be a pebble of love. Ask them to carry it on their person every day, perhaps taking it out at night and reclaiming each morning as a way of recommitting to being a pebble of love that day.

YOUTH PLEDGE OF NONVIOLENCE

Making peace must start within ourselves and in our school. Each of us, teenagers at_____school/parish, commit ourselves as best we can to become nonviolent and peaceable people.

To Respect Self and Others
To respect myself, to affirm others and to avoid uncaring criticism,
hateful words, physical or emotional attacks, negative peer pressure,
and self-destructive behavior, including abuse of alcohol and drugs.

To Communicate Better
To share my feelings honestly, to look for safe ways to express my anger
and other emotions, to work at solving problems peacefully,
and to encourage an open system of communication throughout the school.

To Listen
To listen carefully to one another, especially those who disagree with me,
and to consider others' feelings and needs as valid as my own.

To Forgive
To apologize and make amends when I have hurt another,
to forgive others, and to keep from holding grudges.

To Respect Nature
To treat the environment and all living things with respect and care
and to promote environmental concern in the school.

To Recreate Nonviolently
To select activities and entertainment that strengthen my commitment to nonviolence
and that promote a less violent society, and to avoid social activities that make violence
look exciting, funny or acceptable.

To Act Courageously
To challenge violence in all its forms whenever I encounter it,
whether at home, at school, at work, or in the community, and to stand with others
who are treated unfairly, even if it means standing alone.
"Eliminating violence, one school at a time, starting with our own."

Institute for Peace and Justice
website: www.ipj-ppj.org

"Pebbles of Love Against the Boulders of Violence"

The Scale of Violence and Love

The spirit and forces of violence in our communities and world seem to be in a constant war with the spirit and forces of peace and love. The traditional "scale of justice" is one effective way to symbolize this tension and struggle and how our lives and actions can make a difference in the ongoing transformation of the world.

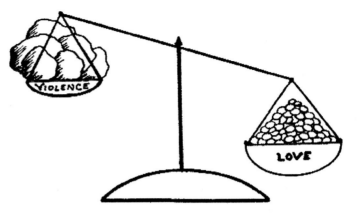

"In the Face of Escalating Violence, Escalate Love"

The "Boulders of Violence"

Illustrated as hard and hurtful boulders, some of the most common and deadly forms of violence are hate violence, domestic violence, the violence of war and terrorism, the violence glorified in the media and in entertainment and sports, and the various forms of institutional violence—racism, economic injustice, sexism. What other boulders of violence would you add to this tray?

Confronting the Boulders

Piled up on a single tray, there are openings among these boulders that represent the opportunities we have to confront directly the violence in our society—by our efforts to change public policy on these issues and to dramatize and protest against the violence. But these boulders can also be confronted indirectly. Every moment of every day we can live our lives in tiny loving ways that help to offset the effects of the boulders of violence on us physically, emotionally, and spiritually. These tiny acts of love, spelled out in the Pledge of Nonviolence and symbolized by tiny pebbles, are part of the solution to the violence that is overwhelming our society and sometimes even our own spirits.

Being a "Pebble of Love"

A pebble is a humble object, much smaller than a boulder. But as a pebble in the hands of God, each of us can become a powerful as well as humble instrument of God's peace in our world. Consider that each day God picks up each of us and places us in a variety of situations, hoping that we will consent to be the instruments of God's peace in those situations. Picture how a pebble dropped in a pool of water sends out many ripples, touching many things. That's what we are in the hands of God. Each tiny act of love sends out many ripples, although we don't always see where all those ripples go and all that they touch. But with the eyes of faith, we believe that our pebbles are powerful when they are united with the love of God poured out in the person of Jesus and all the other prophets and witnesses of faith in history. And together we can be even more powerful pebbles for peace.

Question:
➤ *What can you do each day to be a more powerful pebble of love in the hands of God?*

A LITANY ON THE PEBBLES OF LOVE

In the face of the boulders of disrespect for all who are different,
Let us be pebbles of respect for the dignity and diversity of every person.

In the face of the boulders of having it always my way,
Let us be pebbles of mutuality.

In the face of the boulders of tuning out others,
Let us be pebbles of listening love.

In the face of the boulders of grudges and retaliation,
Let us be pebbles of forgiving love.

In the face of the boulders of using more than our share,
Let us be pebbles of simple sufficiency.

In the face of the boulders of violence against other species and the earth herself,
Let us be pebbles of beauty and respect.

In the face of the boulders of violent entertainment,
Let us be pebbles of playfulness.

In the face of the boulders of discrimination and exploitation because of race, age, gender, or sexual orientation,
Let us be pebbles of solidarity.

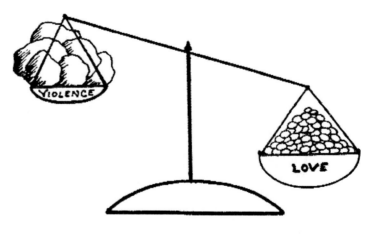

"In the Face of Escalating Violence, Escalate Love"

Chapter 8, Activity 3

Only Forgiveness Can Break the Cycle of Violence

Step 1—Introduction

Among the seven components of the Youth Pledge of Nonviolence, this activity singles out the forgiveness component, because only forgiveness can ultimately break the cycle of violence. Forgiving those who have hurt us is probably the most difficult aspect of Christian love. It could be said that forgiveness is what separates the disciples of Jesus from the "wannabes." Forgiveness is certainly central to the Peace Prayer of Saint Francis (page 184 of the Student Text), which could be used as the opening prayer as well as the final step in this activity. While this activity focuses primarily on interpersonal situations, it could be expanded to include community, national, or international situations. Revisiting the example of Bud Welch and his opposition to capital punishment in Step 4 could open this exploration, if time permits.

This activity would best be done in two or three class periods. The first class would focus on steps 2 and 3, with students finishing step 3 on their own between classes. The second class would focus on steps 4, 5, and 6, with students completing step 5 on their own between classes. With additional time, the suggestion on burying the rock or burning the paper with the name of the grudge could be done as a whole class ritual for completing the experience.

Step 2—The experience of being forgiven

Background

Psychologically, it is easier to consider forgiving others if we remember some of the times when we have been forgiven and how that felt.

Student reflection

Distribute the handout "Being Forgiven and Making Amends" (page 160) and ask students to write their reflections on question 1. You might stimulate more honest reflection by giving an example from your own life.

Discussion

Invite students to share their answers in groups of two or three. If time permits, ask students to share some of their reflections with the whole group, especially on how it feels to be forgiven.

Step 3—Apologizing and making amends

Background

It is also helpful to become more aware of the times we have hurt others before thinking about our own hurts. The more aware we are of our own sinfulness, the more likely we will be to forgive others.

Student reflection

Ask students to write their answers to the questions on "Being Forgiven and Making Amends" (page 160). This might best be completed at home before the next class. At the beginning of the next class, the students could be invited to share in groups of two or three some of what they decided to do.

Step 4—Why forgive?

Reflection

Distribute the handout "On Letting Go of Grudges" (page 161). Revisit the story of Bud Welch and the photo of the cross with "168 Reasons to Love One Another," from Chapter 4, activity 3. Ask students to reflect in writing on questions 1, 2, and 3.

Discussion

Discuss question 1 as a whole group. Invite students to share their answers to question 3 with the whole group. If time permits, ask them to reflect aloud on their answers to question 2 and raise the issue of how forgiveness can be expanded to include community, national, and international situations where forgiveness would help break the cycle of violence.

Step 5—Forgiving

Reflection

If time permits, ask students to begin their answers to question 4. Have them complete their answers on their own between classes.

Decisions and ritual

Invite students to answer question 5 and then to ritualize it personally or with the entire class. Invite them to answer question 6 as well, perhaps sharing their answers with a partner, especially if the ritual will be a group experience.

Step 6—Francis's Peace Prayer

Pray together Saint Francis's Prayer for Peace (page 184 of the Student Text) or sing the first verse of John Foley's version of the Peace Prayer, noting his phrase—"where there's injury, Lord, let forgiveness be my sword." This is an appropriate version because of Francis's own taking up the sword as a young man fighting for Assisi against the town of Perugia and then later going off to battle as a crusader.

BEING FORGIVEN AND MAKING AMENDS

1. Describe a situation in which you were forgiven—what did you do to that person, when and how did they forgive you, and how did it feel to be forgiven?

2. Write the names of all the people you can remember having hurt in some way (in the first column), how you think they felt (second column), and how you could make amends (third column).

Name	How They Felt	How I Could Make Amends

3. Choose one of these persons to address. Now close your eyes and imagine the offended person in front of you. Begin a letter telling that person you are sorry.

4. Then add to your letter what you are going to do to make amends to that person for what you have done to them. Whether or not you mail it, the letter is an important way for you to identify and take responsibility for your actions.

5. Name an actual time and way you will convey your apology and make amends.

ON LETTING GO OF GRUDGES

1. Why is it so hard sometimes to forgive?

2. What do the story of Bud Welch's act of forgiveness and the photo of the cross at the Oklahoma City bombsite say to you about forgiveness?

3. Why should you let go of grudges and forgive?

4. Make a list of all the grudges you have been carrying, with the name of the person(s) who hurt or offended you in some way, how long you have been holding on to that grudge, whether it's time to let go, and what you might say or do to that person or persons to show forgiveness.

Name/Grudge	How Long Ago?	Is It Time to Let Go?	How Could You Forgive?

5. Choose one grudge you are ready to let go of, perhaps write the person's name on a rock and bury it or throw it in a body of water (or write it on a piece of paper and burn the paper), and then let that person know by your words that he/she is forgiven.

6. Is there something else you could do to become a more forgiving person?

Chapter 8, Activity 4

Peacemaking Is Patriotic

Step 1—Introduction

This activity addresses "The Option of Nonviolence" segment (pages 182–184 of the Student Text) and "The Just War Tradition" segment (pages 185–189 of the Student Text) in Chapter 8. The U.S. Catholic Bishops are clear that those who choose to join the military in defense of their country and those who choose the pacifist option and serve their country in other ways are both patriotic. Furthermore, the "Just War Tradition" implies that the Church as a whole and individual Christians have a responsibility to challenge those wars that don't meet the "just war" criteria. But because those who do challenge their government's decisions to go to war are generally labeled as unpatriotic, it is especially important to look at the Church's understanding of the virtue of patriotism and its implications.

This activity invites students to reflect on the Church's teaching on Christian patriotism and on the words and deeds of two persons who considered themselves patriotic peacemakers. Then it challenges the students to formulate their own understanding of patriotism and put it into practice by writing a letter to the president of the United States.

Depending on the length of your class periods, this activity might be better done in two classes, with steps 2 and 3 for the first class and steps 4 and 5 for the second class or step 5 done by students on their own and brought to the next class.

Step 2—Reflections on Christian patriotism

Word association

Ask students to say aloud the words or phrases that come immediately to them when you say the word "patriotism." List these words on newsprint or the board.

Student reflection and discussion

Distribute the handout "Reflections on Christian Patriotism" (page 167), read the first quotation aloud, and ask the students to write their reflections on the questions that follow. Repeat this process for sections 2 and 3 of the handout.

Decisions and sharing

Ask students to answer in writing the two decision items at the bottom of the handout. Invite them to share their answers in groups of two or three. If time permits, invite them to share some of their reflections with the whole class.

Step 3—Amber Amundson's letter to the President

Student reflection

Distribute the handout "Amber Amundson's Letter to the President" (page 168). Ask students to read it silently and then answer the first question.

Discussion

Invite students to share their responses aloud, especially the reasons behind their answers.

Step 4—Breaking the silence

Background

Martin Luther King, Jr., gave his lengthy "When Silence Is Betrayal" speech at Riverside Church in New York City on April 4, 1967, exactly one year to the day before his assassination. It marked his own breaking of the silence on the Vietnam War and created tremendous controversy even within the Civil Rights Movement itself. Many thought that President Johnson's support for civil rights shouldn't be jeopardized by Dr. King's criticizing the president's policy on Vietnam. The excerpts presented on the handout challenge students to examine their own willingness to speak out on important issues in general as well as formulate their own position on war and act on it. This is where the Church's teaching on the Just War Tradition can best be incorporated into the activities for chapter 8.

Dr. King's words

Distribute the student handout "Breaking the Silence" (page 169). As a way of emphasizing each paragraph, read one paragraph at a time, and then have the students read that paragraph again as a whole group. Pause between paragraphs to allow the words to seep in.

Student reflection and discussion

Ask students to write their answers to question 1, perhaps sharing them briefly in pairs. Discuss question 2 as a whole class.

Have students underline those statements they agree with and put parentheses around those with which they disagree. Discuss their answers as a whole group.

Have them write their answers to question 4 in silence.

Question 5 can be incorporated into their letters to the president in step 5.

Step 5—Students' letters to the President

Background options

If you did step 4, this could provide a broader focus for the students' own letters to the president. If you didn't include step 4, then the focus would be the narrower one of responding to current United States policy in the war on terrorism. You also need to decide whether you want the students to turn in their letters for you to read or to keep them private.

Writing the letters

Invite the students to write their letters on their own before the next class. You might encourage them to include some of their religious beliefs that underlie the political actions they are suggesting.

Discussion

If time permits and if students find that sharing their reflections is helpful, you might ask them to share their letters in groups of two or three before turning them in or mailing them.

Ritual and mailing

You might consider some kind of prayer service in which the letters in stamped envelopes are brought forward and placed in a basket and lifted up as an offering of the students' acts for peace.

REFLECTIONS ON CHRISTIAN PATRIOTISM

1. *"The virtue of patriotism means that as citizens we respect and honor our country, but our very love and loyalty make us examine carefully and regularly its role in world affairs asking that it live up to is full potential as an agent of peace with justice for all people"* (U.S. Catholic Bishops, The Challenge of Peace, *1983, #327*).

➤ *What does it mean to "respect and honor our country"? to show "love and loyalty"?*

➤ *How do you concretely do these things?*

➤ *What specifically do you think we should be asking our country to do in order to "live up to its full potential as an agent of peace with justice for all people"?*

➤ *Is this constructive criticism a patriotic or unpatriotic act and why?*

2. *"To teach the ways of peace is not to weaken the nation's will but to be concerned for the nation's soul"* (U.S. Catholic Bishops, The Challenge of Peace, *1983, #304*).

➤ *What do you think the bishops mean by this statement? Why are they concerned for our nation's soul?*

➤ *Is it unpatriotic to have such concerns? Why or why not?*

3. Martin Luther King, Jr., was also concerned about our nation's soul. He helped to create the Southern Christian Leadership Conference, whose motto was "We have come to redeem the soul of America." In 1967, he broke his silence about the Vietnam war and boldly proclaimed: "Never again will I be silent on an issue that is destroying the soul of our nation and destroying thousands and thousands of little children in Vietnam. . . . The time has come for a real prophecy, and I'm willing to go that road" (quoted in Road to Redemption, *p. 14*).

➤ *Do you think the soul of our nation is in jeopardy today? Why or why not?*

4. Decisions. *What do you think you are being called to by these statements and questions?*

➤ *After thinking about all of this, briefly define your own understanding of Christian patriotism:*

AMBER AMUNDSON'S LETTER TO THE PRESIDENT

Amber Amundson thought she was honoring and loving her country and asking it to "live up to its full potential as an agent of peace with justice for all people" when she wrote President George W. Bush after her husband was killed in the terrorist attack on the Pentagon on September 11, 2001. This is what she wrote:

November 24, 2001

Dear President Bush,

My name is Amber Amundson. I am a 28-year-old single mother of two small children. The reason I am a single mother is because my husband was murdered on September 11, while working under your direction. My husband, Craig Amundson, was an active duty multimedia illustrator for your Deputy Chief of Staff of Personnel Command, who was also killed.

I am not doing well. I am hurt that the U.S. is moving forward in such a violent manner. I do not hold you responsible for my husband's death, but I do believe you have a responsibility to listen to me and please hear my pain. I do not like unnecessary death. I do not want anyone to use my husband's death to perpetuate violence. So, Mr. President, when you say that vengeance is needed so that the victims of 9/11 do not die in vain, could you please exclude Craig Amundson from your list of victims used to justify further attacks? I do not want my children to grow up thinking that the reason so many people died following the September 11 attack was because of their father's death. I want to show them a world where we love and not hate, where we forgive and not seek out vengeance.

Please Mr. Bush, help me honor my husband. He drove to the Pentagon with a Visualize World Peace bumper sticker on his car every morning. He raised our children to understand humanity and not fight to get what you want. When we buried my husband, an American flag was laid over his casket. My children believe the American flag represents their dad. Please let that representation be one of love, peace and forgiveness. I am begging you, for the sake of humanity and my children, to stop killing. Please find a nonviolent way to bring justice to the world.

Sincerely,
Amber Amundson

Questions:

➤ *Do you consider Amber's letter patriotic or unpatriotic? Why?*

➤ *What would your own letter to the president say about responding to the threats of terrorism and what you want this country to be?*

BREAKING THE SILENCE

From "When Silence Is Betrayal" by Martin Luther King, Jr., April 4, 1967

"A time comes when silence is betrayal. Even when pressed by the demands of inner truth, men [sic] do not easily assume the task of opposing their government's policy, especially in time of war. Nor does the human spirit move without great difficulty against all the apathy of conformist thought within one's own bosom and in the surrounding world. Moreover, when the issues at hand seem as perplexing as they often do in the case of dreadful conflict, we are always on the verge of being mesmerized by uncertainty. But we must move on.

"Some of us who have already begun to break the silence of the night have found that the calling to speak is often a vocation of agony, but we must speak. We must speak with all the humility that is appropriate to our limited vision, but we must speak. For we are deeply in need of a new way beyond the darkness that seems so close around us.

"We are called to speak for the weak, for the voiceless, for the victims of our nation, for those it calls 'enemy,' for no document from human hands can make these humans any less our brothers. I think of them, too, because it is clear to me that there will be no meaningful solution until some attempt is made to know them and hear their broken cries.

"A true revolution of values will lay hand on the world order and say of war, 'This way of settling differences is not just.' A nation that continues year and year to spend more money on military defense than on programs of social uplift is approaching spiritual death.

"This call for a worldwide fellowship that lifts neighborly concern beyond one's tribe, race, class, and nation is in reality a call for an all-embracing and unconditional love for all humankind. We can no longer afford to worship the God of hate or bow before the altar of retaliation. The oceans of history are made turbulent by the ever-rising tides of hate. History is cluttered with the wreckage of nations and individuals that pursued this self-defeating path of hate."

Questions:

1. How do you feel about Dr. King's urging you to speak out against war?

2. Why did Dr. King oppose the war in Vietnam and modern war in general?

3. What do agree with in his speech and why? What do you disagree with and why?

4. Do you think you participate in the "silence of betrayal"? Betrayal of what?

5. As a Catholic, what do you think needs to be said and done at this point in the current war on terrorism?

Chapter 9

Justice and Work

(See pages 203–226 of *Catholic Social Teaching*)

Work has two dimensions—the objective (what is produced) and the subjective (the workers themselves). Of these two dimensions, the subjective is more important—after all, work exists for the sake of people, not the other way around. The Church acknowledges this in stressing the rights of workers.

Chapter 9, Activity 1

"Free the Children"

Step 1—Introduction

This activity is designed to give students a greater understanding of the issue of child labor that is acknowledged in the Student Text on pages 204–205. More importantly, it provides the opportunity for both individual and group action, challenging students to put Catholic social teaching into practice.

If you want specific information on how the Free the Children chapter in St. Cloud, Minnesota, planned and conducted their "Sweatshop for a Day" experience, contact the Center for Service Learning and Social Change in St. Cloud (320-259-5480).

The Free the Children website—www.freethechildren.org—has a wealth of information and action suggestions on the overall campaign and on the general issue of child labor.

Step 2—Present the issue

Background information

To put this specific campaign in a broader context, present some background information on the general issue of child labor, perhaps asking several students to research the issue and share what they learn with the whole class.

The "Free the Children" campaign

Distribute the handout "Free the Children" (page 173) and have students read the paragraphs on Iqbal Masih and Craig Kielburger. Supplement this information with what they may know and what you research on the Free the Children website.

The responses of others

Have students read the paragraph on "100,000 more youth join." Supplement this information with any additional information you or the students discover.

Step 3—Reflection and decisions

Reflection

Have students write their answers to the first three questions under "And you?" perhaps sharing their answers in groups of two or three.

Brainstorm action possibilities

Ask students for their answers to the first three questions to see how many might be interested in doing something about the issue. Brainstorm additional action possibilities.

Decisions

Decide with your class whether they want to respond as a group and begin creating an action plan. If a group action is not a possibility, encourage students to consider responding as individuals and to pray for all those involved. Ask them to write their decision(s) to question 4.

FREE THE CHILDREN

Iqbal Masih

In 1986 in Pakistan, four-year-old Iqbal Masih was sold by his indebted parents into forced labor at a carpet factory. Iqbal worked fourteen hours a day, six days a week. One day when he was ten years old, Iqbal snuck out of the factory and went to a rally where he was so inspired that he gave a speech about his hard life. He refused to go back to the factory and started speaking out against child labor. Because Iqbal's efforts helped to free thousands of other child slaves, he was murdered in 1995 at age twelve.

Craig Kielburger

In Toronto, Ontario, twelve-year-old Craig Kielburger wasn't really a social change type person, but one day he saw a newspaper article about Iqbal Masih entitled, "Boy, 12, Who Spoke Out, Murdered." It intrigued him enough that he started reading about child labor. Eventually he talked with some of his classmates. Within a few weeks, twenty of them decided to form a group and call it Free the Children (FTC). They sent petitions on child labor to government and business leaders, set up public displays, gave speeches, and raised money through car washes and walk-a-thons.

100,000 more youth join

By 2002, FTC had over 100,000 members in thirty-five countries, mostly in small school, church, or neighborhood groups. As part of their FTC efforts, Catholic high school youth in the FTC chapter in St. Cloud, Minnesota, created a "Sweatshop for a Day" event. For thirteen hours, they sewed hundreds of cloth bags and then filled them with school supplies donated by their classmates. They sent these to the FTC headquarters in Toronto, where they were sent on to schools in poor countries. Participants got to experience in a tiny way what these child laborers were forced to do every day. Free the Children continues to inspire other young people to join in this struggle. You can read about these efforts and find out how you might help by visiting their website—www.freethechildren.org.

And you?

1. What do you think of what Iqbal and Craig did?

2. What could you and your classmates do to oppose child labor?

3. Would you be willing to start or be part of a Free the Children group in your school? Why or why not?

4. What are you going to do about this injustice?

Chapter 9, Activity 2

"To Cross or Not to Cross, That Is the Question"

Step 1—Introduction

This activity is designed to challenge students to apply Catholic social teaching to difficult social and economic situations and make personal decisions about their own participation in what might be unjust situations. It addresses the segment of the Student Text on "The Rights and Duties of Workers," pages 210–218, and especially pages 215–216 on "The Right of Association."

Step 2—Church teaching on the rights of workers and their right to unionize

Reflection

Have students read pages 215–216 of the Student Text on "The Right of Association," perhaps putting a plus (+) sign by those passages that they agree with, a minus (-) sign by those passages they disagree with, and a question mark (?) by those they aren't sure about or don't understand.

Discussion

Going down each of the paragraphs in the Student Text, find those passages which were the most challenging or confusing to the class, solicit their reasons for disagreeing, and/or find the specific points they didn't understand and address these. If there isn't time to focus on all these points, be sure to focus on this one: Do you agree that unions are a positive step toward economic justice? Why or why not?

Step 3—Case studies

Reflection on the situations in the text

If time permits, use some or all of the seven situations on page 216 of the Student Text as the basis for student reflection. You might do this in a large space where one end of the open space represents "definitely agree" and the other end represents "definitely disagree." Read each situation and ask students to locate themselves at that point on the continuum which represents their opinion. You might occasionally ask why some students took the position they did. At the end, you might ask what generalizations could be made from the positions the students took.

Reflection on the essay

Distribute the student handout "To Cross or Not to Cross: The Moral Dilemma of the Picket Line" (page 178) and have students read the article. Ask if there are any clarification questions about what the author was saying. Ask the students whether they agree with the two highlighted portions, especially the first—would they generally give the benefit of the doubt to the workers?

Taking a position

Ask students to write their answers to the first question. Consider having students take their position physically on a continuum between "definitely cross" to "definitely not cross," or role-play the situation. Choose some students who agree with the workers to represent those on the picket line, perhaps with signs urging others to honor the picket line. Have the rest of the class approach the picket line and pause. Encourage those on the picket line to appeal to the others not to cross. Encourage the others to state their own concerns about the situation. After the dialogue has gone on for a few minutes, ask those approaching the picket line to make a decision—to cross or not to cross and then implement their decision as if this were a real-life situation.

Reflection on the experience

Ask students how they felt about what happened and what they learned about themselves and about situations like these. Discuss as a whole class the second question after the article.

Step 4 (Optional)—Participating in boycotts

Background

The case studies challenged students to think through the issue of supporting workers striking for greater justice in the workplace. This step applies that thinking to current campaigns for greater justice in the workplace.

Research

Have students do research on the Internet about current economic boycotts, especially those relating to products that touch their lives—e.g., sweatshops for shoes and clothes (e.g., Nike shoes), fast-food chains (e.g., Taco Bell), and retail stores (e.g., Wal-Mart). Co-op America maintains a detailed list of consumer boycotts on their website—www.coopamerica.org. You might also consider inviting a representative from a local union to speak to your class and/or show the *Frontline* video on Wal-Mart.

Discussion and decision

Have students report on their research, and decide as a class whether to join one of these campaigns and which one. If the decision is to join one, create a plan that would include identifying others who should be asked to help, how to publicize the project, and a timeline for completing the project.

"To Cross or Not to Cross: The Moral Dilemma of the Picket Line"

Background:

Grocery workers in St. Louis went out on strike at one chain and were locked out of two other chains in September 2003. The main issues were wages (the companies offered a twenty-five-cent/hour raise) and health care (workers would have to pay more of their coverage). This article details the situation.

In the late 1800s, Mother Jones was defending the rights of coal miners in Virginia. If Mother Jones were alive today, one wonders how she would respond to the complexity of our twenty-first-century labor issues. At the turn of the twentieth century, working conditions were not only miserable but dangerous. There was no such thing as a minimum wage, and workers often were held hostage by "company towns" that owned everything from grocery stores to schools. Few miners lived long enough to collect a pension. For generations, families of immigrant workers who were unionized by Mother Jones would never have dreamed of crossing a picket line. . . . The right to organize—and strike—was a hard-won victory, and no one questions it today. Owners and managers are highly organized by definition, and the unions provide an essential balance to that power.

*Still, workers and management are not natural enemies as they once were. They function in an economic partnership, and it is rare that one or the other stands in a position of absolute justice. **We might grant the benefit of the doubt to unionized workers**, but that does not let us off the hook. We still have to make a moral judgment about how far to support the workers' claims and, ultimately, whether to cross picket lines.*

Like other moral choices, this one requires that we weigh a number of factors. Unlike their nineteenth-century colleagues, many unionized workers today are highly skilled professionals. Their struggle is not usually about a living wage and basic human dignity. More often it is about vacation days, sharing health care costs, job security, and work rules. It is about making a good standard of living better.

In making a choice about where to shop, we have to consider workers' demands in light of actual economic conditions. We have to weigh the impact on the public, especially if work stoppages affect basic services such as transportation, health care and public safety. We also have to take into account the executives' salaries, and the impact of global competition. We have to consider owners' use of the media to influence public opinion and their ability to wait out a strike by hiring temporary workers or shifting revenue.

Finally, we need to be mindful of the irony that those who need unions most, namely unskilled workers who make minimum wage and receive no benefits, often have no hope of belonging to one of them.

I thought about all of these things many times in the past few weeks as I looked at striking and locked-out workers. I reached a decision, and I stuck by it. This particular labor dispute may be nearing an end, but there will be others, and I'll have to consider the facts and come to a decision again. Next time, I might choose differently.

(Excerpts from an article by Fr. Charles Bouchard, Aquinas Institute, St. Louis.)

Questions:

➤ *Would you cross the picket line in this case? Why or why not?*

➤ *In what kinds of situations would you cross a picket line and in what kinds of situations would you not cross?*

➤ *Research the rule of Mother Jones in the Virginia coalminers strikes in the nineteenth century.*

Chapter 9, Activity 3

Work and Money: A "Just Wage" and You

Step 1—Introduction

This activity is designed, first, to challenge students to recognize the implications of Catholic social teaching on a "just wage" and then put this teaching into practice. As the Student Text presents it, the activity proceeds from the Church's teaching (see pages 211–212) to the research task of "Planning a Budget" (page 213). Students are then challenged to identify those in their nation and in their local area who do not receive a "just wage." Finally, they are invited to respond to this injustice in some concrete way.

If time permits, and as a transition to reflecting on the purpose of work in activity 4, step 6 challenges students to reflect on their own experiences of money and financial security and on the importance of these in their lives now and in the future. It ends with biblical reflection and personal decisions.

Step 2—Church teaching on a "just wage"

Reflection

Have students read the section in their text on "Right to a Just Wage," pages 211–212, and put a plus (+) sign by those statements they agree with, a minus (-) sign by those they want to challenge, and a question mark (?) by those statements they don't understand.

Discussion

Take each paragraph, one at a time, and ask the students to explain their ratings. Discuss those that are particularly challenging or confusing to students.

Step 3—"Planning a Budget"

Clarification

Make sure students understand what the activity on page 213 of the Student Text is calling for, what each of the items under "Basic Expenses" includes, and when they are to report back.

Research teams

Consider the possibility of students working in teams of two or three to do the research, as a way of promoting cooperation/community and improving the quality of the research.

Reporting

Compare the numbers that the students come up with and their answers to the first four questions at the bottom of the page. Save the last question for step 5.

Step 4—Who are the victims of this injustice?

Group brainstorm

Recalling what they learned in chapter 7 on poverty, make three lists of what groups of people, perhaps also the size of their numbers—in the United States, around the world, and then especially in their own local area—are victims of this injustice.

Personal connections

Ask each student to make a list of which of these people they are connected with in some way through school, church, neighborhood, sports, and/or other activities. Then ask them to identify people they know personally who are victims of this injustice. You might invite them to share their lists in groups of two or three, perhaps in their research teams if you used them.

Step 5—Action decisions

Group brainstorm

Starting with their answers to question 5 on "Planning a Budget," page 213, brainstorm and list a variety of action possibilities for remedying this injustice.

Decisions

Discuss the possibility of a group action. If students want to do this, create a plan, including a timeline, and assign responsibilities. If students prefer individual actions, invite them to choose one and create a personal plan. Encourage them to share their ideas with others, especially with those students who want to do something similar.

Step 6—"Just a 'Just Wage' or More?"

Background

As a prelude to activity 4 on the purpose of work, the handout on "Just a 'Just Wage' or More?" (page 183) challenges the students to examine the importance of money and financial security as life goals. It begins with their own experiences, because generally what young people want in life is profoundly affected by their own and their family's experience, especially in matters of money and financial security. Depending on time, responding to the first three sets of questions might best be done by the students on their own before class.

Personal reflection

Distribute the handout and ask students to reflect in writing on the first three sets of questions. If time permits, you might ask the students to share with the whole class or in groups of two or three what they learned about themselves in responding to these questions.

Biblical reflection

Read the two statements of Jesus and ask students to write their reflections, perhaps sharing their reflections in pairs or as a whole group. You might also read the parable of the landowner and the workers in his vineyard (Matthew 20:1–16) and ask students whether they think it was "just" for the landowner to pay the last workers the same daily wage as the first workers.

Discussion and decisions

After this whole consideration of a "just wage" and students' experiences and goals with money, discuss as a whole group whether they think it is just to receive more than a "just wage" and why. Then invite students to reflect on the last question on the handout and write their response. If small group sharing has been effective, you might invite them to share their response in groups of two or three.

"Just a 'Just Wage' or More?"

As you think about your future, a career, and what you want in life, money is a huge factor. Some degree of financial security is an important part of a "just wage." But the big question is how much is enough? How important are money and financial security as you make decisions about your career and about the money you have right now?

1. Your family's experience

The importance of money and financial security in your life depends in part on your family's experience.

➤ *How financially secure would you say your family is?*

➤ *How important is financial security to your parent(s)? Why? To you? Why?*

2. Your own experience with money

The ways you use your money in the future will be affected by how you use it now.

➤ *How much of your money do you spend on yourself? What do you spend it on?*

➤ *How much do you save? What are you saving for?*

➤ *How much do you spend on others? What do you buy them?*

➤ *How much do you donate to groups or individuals who need help?*

3. Your needs and wants

Recalling what you learned while "Planning a Budget," answer the following.

➤ *How much money do you think you'll need to make in order to provide for your basic needs as you see them in the future?*

➤ *What else do you want to have and how much more money will it take to provide for these wants?*

4. Jesus' words

➤ *What Jesus challenges us to consider is how important money and financial security really are. What do you think he means when he says . . .*

"No one can serve both money and God"?

"Seek first the Kingdom of God and all these other things will be given to you"?

5. Decisions

➤ *Do you think it is fair to receive more than a "just wage"? Why or why not?*

➤ *Are there any changes you think you should make in how you use your money now? If so, what specific change(s)? If not, why not?*

Chapter 9, Activity 4

Attitudes Toward Work and Workers

Step 1—Introduction

This activity is designed to get students in touch with society's attitudes and their own attitudes toward work and to challenge them to consider more carefully the service dimension of work and how to put this into practice in the present as well as the future. It builds on the "A Christian View of Work" (pages 206–209 of the Student Text) and "Work and You" (pages 218–220 of the Student Text).

Step 2—"Current Attitudes Toward Work and Workers"

"Write the words . . ."

Distribute the handout "Current Attitudes Toward Work and Workers" (page 187) and ask students to read over the statements in item 1 and write down the words that come immediately to their minds. Sample the students' reactions to each of the ten statements and see what emerges, focusing on those comments you think would be most beneficial. Be sure to address the issue of devaluing the worth of the work of women, janitors, and other service professions, especially if your students have attitudes of superiority because of their economic class, race, or ability.

"Overall attitudes"

Ask students to write their thoughts about the questions in item 2 on the handout, "Overall attitudes." Invite them to share some of their thoughts in groups of two or three. Focus the discussion as a whole group on how the students' attitudes compare with those of their parents, their friends, and society in general. Using the Church's teaching in the text as the reference, ask students to compare these attitudes with the Church's teaching.

"Work attitude assessment"

Ask students to rate themselves on the three "1 to 10" pairs. Create a group profile by asking how many students found themselves on the 1–5 range and on the 6–10 range in each pair. Ask them to identify what they think this says about themselves.

Discuss what they think Mother Teresa means by doing tasks "beautifully" and then have them grade themselves. You might again poll the class on how many gave themselves an "A," "B," etc. Ask students to answer the final question in writing, perhaps sharing their answers in groups of two or three, before moving to the next step.

Step 3—"Work as co-creating with God . . ."

Discuss with the class the meaning and implications of the quotation of Pope John Paul II in section 4 of the handout. Ask students to write their answer to the first question following the quotation and then share some of their answers either in small groups or with the whole class. Depending on time, you might just ask students to write their answers to questions 2 and 4 without sharing them with others. But it would be good to have them share their answers to the third question with at least one other person, as a way of mutual edification and accountability.

Step 4—Prayerful conclusion

Read aloud one or more of the three quotations on page 212 of the Student Text. Invite spontaneous prayers from the class in response to these readings.

CURRENT ATTITUDES TOWARD WORK AND WORKERS

1. Write words that come to your mind when you read each of these statements

"Will work for food," his ragged poster read.

"Get a job!" the passerby shouted.

"The working poor," the story featured.

"I can't afford to retire," the sixty-five-year-old lamented.

"Does this job include benefits?" the job-seeker asked.

"Medicaid Slashed," the headline proclaimed.

"How do they expect me to pay for childcare, transportation, and health insurance, plus all my other bills, on this $7.00 an hour job!" the single mother screamed in frustration.

"That's women's work," the young man protested.

"Women Still Get Paid 2/3 of What Men Do," the headline stated.

"That's the janitor's job," the student argued.

2. Overall attitudes

➤ *Based on your reactions to these statements, how would you describe your overall attitudes toward work, working people, and the unemployed? How do your attitudes compare to those of your family and close friends? to those of society in general?*

3. Work attitude assessment

➤ *In terms of the work you are currently doing at school, at home, on the job, in your community, how would you rate yourself on a scale of 1 to 10 on the following pairs.*

1	2	3	4	5	6	7	8	9	10

I do the least amount that is necessary   *I go beyond what is asked of me*

1	2	3	4	5	6	7	8	9	10

I'm negative and complain a lot   *I'm joyful and positive about what I do*

1	2	3	4	5	6	7	8	9	10

I think about myself first   *I'm careful about how my work affects others*

➤ *In describing our work as something we do for God and for Christ, Mother Teresa says that we should "try to do it as beautifully as possible." What grade (from "A" to "F") would you give yourself on how beautifully you do the various tasks of your life?*

➤ *As you think about all these tasks, what would you say are your main goals in doing them?*

4. Work as co-creating with God, as service to humanity

Pope John Paul II wrote that ". . . men [and women], created in the image of God, share by their work in the activity of the Creator" and that "the purpose of work is to fulfill our own humanity and to benefit the humanity of those our work serves."

1. What are some of the ways you are already using your skills and interests to benefit others?

2. How do you envision putting your skills and interests in the service of others in the future?

3. What could you do right now—at home, at school, on the job, at church, or in the community—to be of greater service?

4. If we are truly are "co-creators" with God, what is it that you would like to create with your life?

Chapter 10

Justice and the Environment

(See pages 229–249 of *Catholic Social Teaching*)

W hen God created the world, he declared it to be "good." Human beings occupy the highest place in creation. With this gift comes the responsibility for stewardship of God's creation—the environment. The three activities in this chapter draw their inspiration from the life and words of naturalist John Muir as well as Francis of Assisi and Native Americans like Chief Seattle.

Chapter 10, Activity 1

Growing in Love and Delight

Stewardship of the earth begins with a friendship with the earth

Step 1—Words of John Muir

John Muir, the great U.S. naturalist and original advocate for our national park system, spent a lifetime delighting in and protecting creation and concluded that "knowledge alone will not protect nature, nor will ethics, for by themselves they do not arouse motivation strong enough to transform the exploitative patterns to which we have become accustomed. The protection of nature must be rooted in love and delight, in religious experience."

This first activity focuses on the need to "love and delight" in nature.

Note: Activities 1 and 2 of this unit ask students to let themselves become vulnerable. Depending on the amount of trust in your classroom, these activities might be difficult for some students, especially for students who can't connect emotionally with the ideas.

Step 2—Background on the current crisis and need for a new human-earth relationship

This fundamental theme of Catholic social teaching presents an enormous challenge. We live in such a consumeristic society that we have failed to understand what God intended for the earth, what Francis celebrated, and what Chief Seattle warned us about— that the earth does not belong to us; we belong to the earth. The writings of Thomas Berry are especially helpful in understanding how much is at stake in this issue (see the Student Text for specific manifestations of this crisis, pages 230–231).

Of all the issues we are concerned with at present, the most basic issue, in my estimation, is that of human-earth relations. . . . Our ultimate failure as humans is to become not a crowning glory of the earth, but the instrument of its degradation. We have contaminated the air, the water, the soil; we have dammed the rivers, cut down the rain forests, destroyed animal habitat on an extensive scale. We have driven the great blue whale and a multitude of animals almost to extinction. We have caused the land to be eroded, the rain to be acid. We have killed ten thousand lakes as habitat for fish.

We are playing for high stakes, the beauty and grandeur and even the survival of the earth in its life-giving powers. From being admired and even worshipped as a mode of divine presence, the earth has become despoiled by the human presence in great urban population centers and in centers of industrial exploitation. . . .

Once a creature of earthly providence, we are now extensively in control of this providence. We now have extensive power over the ultimate destinies of the planet, the power of life and death over many of its life systems. . . .

No adequate scale of action can be expected until the human community is able to act in some unified way to establish a functional relation with the earth process, which itself does not recognize national boundaries. . . . Our challenge is to create a new sense of what it is to be human. It is to transcend not only national limitations, but even our species isolation, to enter into the larger community of living species.
(Thomas Berry, The Dream of the Earth, *pages 42–43, 50–51).*

This new human-earth community has tremendous potential for enhancing all parties, but it won't happen until we humans become more like Francis and Chief Seattle and begin to look upon the earth and all its resources and species as kin, as a community we need to get to know, enjoy, and treasure as we do other good friends.

Step 3—Introduce the twelve ways for growing in love and delight

Distribute the handout "12 Ways to Become Friends With the Earth" (page 193–194). This handout identifies twelve ways for growing in appreciation, friendship, and care of the earth. Some of the items include suggestions for putting the ideas into practice. The questions on the handout are designed to stimulate the students' imaginations as to how to live out each way. While this process is really a lifelong activity and can only be introduced during this unit, students who have a good experience with the process during this study will be encouraged to extend it beyond the unit and term.

Step 4—The first four ways for becoming friends with the earth

Have students answer the questions connected with the first four ways in a journal or notebook. Invite the students to share their answers in pairs. Perhaps have students share some of their answers with the whole class, one step at a time. Their answers for questions 2 and 3 will help them decide what aspect of nature they will speak for in the next activity.

Step 5—Way five on making amends with the earth and her Creator

Have students answer question 5. Invite the students to share their answers in pairs. Perhaps have students share some of their answers with the whole class. Their answers will also help them in the next activity.

Step 6—Personal decisions, implementation, reflection, and reports

Ask each student to make a decision about what one specific way they will start or deepen their friendship with the earth. Have them write that decision in their journal or notebook and perhaps share it with their partner as in the earlier steps. Later, encourage them to write about what they did and how it affected them after implementing their decision. Set a time for students to report on what they did and how it affected them.

12 Ways to Become Friends with the Earth

Each of the following ways has questions to help you explore how you might put that way into practice. Use these ways as guides each time you want to explore the beauty and healing power of creation, your place in creation, and how to protect and share creation with others. Write your responses to each question in a notebook or journal.

1. See the faces of the earth

➤ *What are some of the earth's "faces" (e.g., sunrise and sunset) that you enjoy? When, where, and how do you or could you see these and other faces of the earth more fully?*

2. Learn her names and stories

➤ *What are some of your favorite species of animals, trees, flowers? How could you find out more about them? How are you learning about the story of the earth and/or the universe as a whole?*

3. "Commune-icate" with the earth

➤ *Do you have some special places you like to visit where you feel close to nature? What makes them special for you? How are you present to the earth in those places? What are you learning from the different species there? When could you visit them more regularly?*

4. Touch the earth

➤ *What are some ways you can touch the earth more carefully with your hands and/or feet? Do you have or help with a garden? What opportunity do you have for hiking or nature walks?*

5. Make amends with the earth

➤ *What are some of the ways you have hurt the earth and how can you more sincerely and effectively apologize and make amends for those hurts?*

6. Eat with the earth

➤ *Have you ever thought of having a picnic with the earth, perhaps just you and the earth or you and another special friend? This would be a time when you would just enjoy and communicate with the earth. Where would be some good places for you to have these picnics? What would be appropriate foods to bring for such picnics? Some people like to bring fruit from the earth and some bread that they bake themselves, so that both are each contributing something to the meal.*

7. Sing and dance with the earth

➤ *What songs or dances do you know that you can sing with the earth? What songs does the earth sing that you could listen to more carefully?*

8. Praise the earth and her Creator

➤ *What Psalms, other biblical passages, and/or other hymns of praise do you or could you say regularly? You might even consider writing your own psalm, song, or love letter.*

9. Exchange gifts with the earth

➤ *What gifts do you receive from the earth? What gifts are you giving or could you give to the earth? Lots of people plant trees as a way of giving something back to the earth. Can you do this or contribute money to help others do this? For suggestions check the website of Global ReLeaf: www.americanforests.org*

10. Protect the earth; stand in defense of creation

➤ *What are you doing individually and as a school or faith community to protect the earth? Be sure to consider both lifestyle decisions and social change activities addressing political and economic institutions/policies that harm the earth. Check the websites of groups like the Sierra Club, the Nature Conservancy, and the National Wildlife Federation.*

11. Make your friendship/commitment explicit

➤ *Write a letter of friendship to the earth in which you celebrate her, tell her what you like best about her, thank her for her gifts, apologize for hurting her, name how you will protect her more, and anything else you want to say. Create an "I Love the Earth" book of your photographs, postcards, and reflections.*

12. Share your friend/concern with others

➤ *How can you become a public witness ("prophet") on behalf of the earth? What about raising some of these issues at school and/or with your faith community, or perhaps an article for a school/church newsletter and/or a letter to the editor of your local newspaper? Share your "I Love the Earth" book with friends.*

Chapter 10, Activity 2

Speaking for the Earth

Step 1—Introduction

This activity builds on the first five ways in the "12 Ways to Become Friends With the Earth" handout (used in activity 1), and provides an opportunity for each student to become a spokesperson or prophet for the earth as part of being a "steward" or protector of the earth (ways ten and twelve). This activity is adapted from Joanna Rogers Macy's "Council of All Beings" process in her book *Thinking Like a Mountain: Toward a Council of All Beings*. *Note:* As mentioned in activity 1, this activity asks students to let themselves become vulnerable and open up with others in ways they are not used to doing.

Step 2—Explain the worksheet and process

Distribute the handout "Speaking for the Earth" (page 198) and explain that each student will become a spokesperson or prophet for some life form addressing their classmates as this life form by reading the answers they write to the four questions on the worksheet. The gathering at which each student will speak is called a "Council of All Beings," at which each life form the students choose will address their human classmates in a circle or "council."

Step 3—Choose and research the life form or aspect of creation for whom they will speak

Ask each student to choose an animal, plant, or other part of the earth family that they especially love, that has been abused by humans, and that they want to protect. If they have any difficulty in deciding for whom to speak, have them recall their answers in the previous activity to the questions for ways two and three in the "12 Ways to Become Friends With the Earth."

Depending on the amount of time available for this activity, have the students research their life forms and write out their answers to the four questions on the worksheet, in preparation for reciting them at the Council of All Beings. If necessary, give them some examples of how to answer the questions, using your own life form or part of the earth family as an example.

Step 4—Draw a picture of their life form or aspect of the earth

Ask the students to draw a picture of their special part of the earth family on the opposite side of their worksheet. Because they may want to redraw their picture, it is best to have them draw their picture on a separate sheet of paper or cardboard and then attach their final product to the opposite side of their worksheet. This picture will be the "mask" behind which each student will address the Council of All Beings.

This creative aspect of the activity may be resisted by some of the students, but encourage them to try it, no matter how good or bad they may see themselves as artists. Again, your own picture may be helpful.

Step 5—The Council of All Beings

As a whole class or in smaller groups (with a facilitator for each group), have each student, one at a time, come to the front, sit in a chair with their worksheet "mask" in front of their face, and read their statement on the other side.

After each statement, the rest of the class/group responds:

> *"We hear you, _____. We are sorry for what we have done to you and promise to treat you more carefully from now on.*

Step 6—Follow-up discussion

To conclude, ask the students how they felt about being a spokesperson for some part of the earth's family and what they learned from this activity.

Step 7—Personal decisions on how to better protect the earth

Based on what they heard from each life form at the Council and on their own pleading on behalf of the earth, as well as the suggestions offered in the Student Text (pages 239–240), have each student decide one thing they will do to make amends to the earth and better protect the earth (items five and ten in the twelve-way process); record this decision in their journal or notebook; and then perhaps report back a week later on how they implemented their decision.

Step 8—Expressing our friendship/commitment to the earth

As a way of implementing way eleven in the twelve-way process for becoming friends with the earth, have the students brainstorm a variety of suggestions for expressing this friendship, beginning with those identified in way eleven—a letter of friendship or an "I Love the Earth" book. Writing a poem, drawing a picture, and creating a photographic display are some additional possibilities, but see what the students suggest before adding these possibilities.

SPEAKING FOR THE EARTH

I speak for the _____

Name the animal, plant, or other life form or part of the earth family that you especially love and want to protect.

What it's like to be me:

Describe your size and shape, how you move, how you sound or smell or feel.

What some people have done to me:

Describe how people have misused or hurt you.

Why I'm so special:

What is it that people love about you? How do you make life better for humans and other creatures?

How I want you to treat me from now on:

Tell the humans how you want them to treat you; be specific.

Others respond:

"We hear you, _____. We are sorry for what we have done to you and promise to treat you more carefully from now on."

Chapter 10, Activity 3

Finding God in Creation

Step 1—Introduction

This activity is designed to provide John Muir's "religious experience"—to deepen students' sense of God's presence and goodness in all of creation, their sense of prayerfulness and gratitude to God, and their sense of being called by the Creator of the universe to be "stewards" of God's creation. It will provide another opportunity to implement ways one and three in the "12 Ways to Become Friends With the Earth" and to implement way eight. Finally, this activity will help students realize the power of beauty to gentle us down and heal us.

Step 2—Reflection

Illustrating the passage(s)

Choose one or more of the following reflective passages, create a poster with the words that are chosen, and select one or more pictures for each, and/or invite student volunteers to illustrate them.

"The heavens declare the glory of God and the firmament proclaims God's handiwork" *(Psalm 19:1).*

Other Psalms to consider: 8, 65, 104, 136, 145, 147, 148.

"The protection of nature must be rooted in love and delight, in religious experience" *(John Muir).*

"My profession is to be always on the alert to find God in nature, to know God's lurking places . . ." *(Henry David Thoreau).*

"The first peace, which is the most important, is that which comes within the souls of people when they realize their relationship, their oneness, with the universe and all its powers; and when they realize that at the center of the universe dwells the Great Spirit, and that this center is really everywhere; it is within each of us" (Chief Black Elk in The Sacred Pipe: Black Elk's Account of the Seven Rites of the Oglala Sioux).

"Savor creation as the revelation and celebration of God's love" (the verse on the Savor Creation greeting cards from the Institute for Peace and Justice).

Praying the passage(s)

Display the poster(s) in a prominent place and repeat the words prayerfully at the beginning of class.

Step 3—"You will find Me in nature"

Identifying places of beauty

Have students identify some place in or around their home that they enjoy for its beauty. Or encourage them to create a place of beauty, even if it is only a single picture in their room. Next, have students identify a favorite place of beauty in their neighborhood or wider community that they can visit regularly. If they can see the sunrise and/or the sunset from any of these places, encourage them to try these times as God's "primetime revelations."

Using the student handout in one of these places

For at least three days and preferably a full week, encourage students to spend at least ten to twenty minutes each day at one of these places of beauty. Have them use the student handout "You Will Find Me in Nature . . . " (page 202) items one and two, as a way of focusing their attention during these visits.

Giving thanks and praise

Encourage students to do item three on the handout "You Will Find Me in Nature . . ." as the conclusion of their daily encounters with God in nature.

Step 4—Follow-up

Sharing

Invite students to share what they experienced and learned during their visits, perhaps in pairs before sharing with the whole class.

Concluding invitation

Encourage students to place themselves in places of beauty often, to add prayer as a dimension of their presence there, and to keep a journal of their thoughts and feelings about these times and places. Encourage them to revisit "12 Ways to Become Friends With the Earth," perhaps once a week, preferably on Sunday, the time when Scripture says God rested and savored creation. Make this a day of savoring creation, thanking and praising the Creator, and recommitting to ways ten and twelve to protect the earth.

Praying the posters

Return to the poster(s) created in step 2 periodically in the weeks ahead, as a way of reinforcing the lessons from this activity.

Step 5—Litany of Repentance

Introductory note

While the quoted passages on the handout have long been attributed to Chief Seattle as his letter to the president of the United States in 1854, it is now thought to be something written in the 1970s. Whatever its origin, it is widely quoted as a clear expression of the attitudes of Native Americans toward the earth.

Litany

Distribute the student handout "Litany of Repentance" (pages 203–204) and read it prayerfully, with a different student reading each of the passages from the Letter of Chief Seattle and the whole group responding each time.

"YOU WILL FIND ME IN NATURE. ENJOY IT AND THEN THANK ME."

Love, God

1. *If you need some words to help you focus, read these slowly several times and then just be there quietly appreciating what God has created for you.*

> *"The first peace, which is the most important, is that which comes within the souls of people when they realize their relationship, their oneness, with the universe and all its powers; and when they realize that at the center of the universe dwells the Great Spirit, and that this center is really everywhere; it is within each of us."*
>
> —Black Elk

Be still and know that I am God, here with you in the midst of My awesome creation. Savor it in silence. And listen for My Spirit speaking.

2. *What did you learn about the Creator here?*

3. *On the back of this sheet, write God a letter, prayer, psalm, or poem thanking and praising the Creator for his gifts of Creation. If you need help getting started, read Psalm 148 and maybe rewrite it in your own words.*

LITANY OF REPENTANCE

Based on Chief Seattle's 1854 Letter to the U.S. President

The Great Chief in Washington sends word that he wishes to buy our land. . . . We will consider your offer. For we know that if we do not sell, the white man may come with guns and take our land. . . .

For the fear and intimidation we inflicted and continue to inflict on others, we ask forgiveness, Creator God.

Every part of this earth is sacred to my people. Every shining pine needle, every sandy shore, every mist in the dark woods, every clearing, and humming insect is holy in the memory and experience of my people. The sap which courses through the trees carries the memories of the red man. . . . We are part of this earth and it is part of us. The perfumed flowers are our sisters; the deer, the horse, the great eagle, these are our brothers. The rocky crests, the juices of the meadows, the body heat of the pony, and humans—all belong to the same family.

For the times we have not recognized our unity with the rest of creation, we ask forgiveness, Creator God.

We will consider your offer to buy our land. But it will not be easy. For this land is sacred to us. . . . This shining water that moves in the streams and rivers is not just water but the blood of our ancestors. If we sell you land, you must remember that it is sacred, and you must teach your children that it is sacred. . . .

For our lack of appreciation for the holiness and sacredness of creation, we ask forgiveness, Creator God.

The rivers are our brothers, they quench our thirst. The rivers carry our canoes and feed our children. If we sell you our land, you must remember and teach your children that the rivers are our brothers, and yours; and you must henceforth give the rivers the kindness you would give any brother. . . .

For the times we have polluted the waters of our land and not treated them with kindness, we ask forgiveness, Creator God.

We know that the white man does not understand our ways. One portion of land is the same to him as the next, for he is a stranger who comes in the night and takes from the land whatever he needs. The earth is not his brother, but his enemy, and when he has conquered it, he moves on. . . . He treats his mother, the earth, and his brother, the sky, as things to be bought, plundered, sold like sheep or bright beads. His appetite will devour the earth and leave behind only a desert. . . .

For the noise we have created and imposed on nature, we ask forgiveness, Creator God

So we will consider your offer to buy the land. If we decide to accept, I will make one condition: the white man must treat the beasts of this land as his brothers. . . . What are humans without the beasts? If all the beasts were gone, humans would die from a great loneliness of spirit. For whatever happens to the beasts soon happens to humans. All things are connected. . . .

For the times we have been greedy and consumed much more than our fair share, we ask forgiveness, Creator God.

> There is no quiet place in the white man's cities. No place to hear the unfurling of leaves in the spring or the rustle of insects' wings. But perhaps it is because I am a savage and do not understand. The clatter only seems to insult the ears. And what is there to life if a person cannot hear the lonely cry of the whippoorwill or the arguments of the frogs around a pond at night? I am a red man and do not understand. The Indian prefers the soft sound of the wind darting over the face of a pond, and the smell of the wind itself, cleansed by a midday rain or scented with the pinon pine.

For our reckless killing of animals, we ask forgiveness, Creator God.

> You must teach your children that the ground beneath their feet is the ashes of our grandparents. So that they will respect the land, tell your children that the earth is rich with the lives of our kin. Teach your children what we have taught our children, that the earth is our mother. . . .

For our failure to teach children reverence for the earth, we ask forgiveness, Creator God.

> Whatever befalls the earth befalls the sons and daughters of the earth. If we spit upon the ground, we spit upon ourselves. This we know. The earth does not belong to us; we belong to the earth. . . . This we know. All things are connected like the blood which unites one family. All things are connected. Whatever befalls the earth befalls the sons and daughters of the earth. Humans did not weave the web of life; we are merely strands in it. Whatever we do to the web, we do to ourselves. . . .

For all the times we have been careless about the earth, as if we owned the earth, we ask forgiveness, Creator God.

> Even the white man, whose God walks and talks with him as friend to friend, cannot be exempt from the common destiny. We may be brothers after all, we shall see. One thing we know, which the white man may one day discover—our God is the same God. You may think now that you own God as you wish to own our land, but you cannot. God is the God of all, and God's compassion is equal for all. This earth is precious to God, and to harm the earth is to heap contempt on its Creator. The whites too shall pass; perhaps sooner than all other tribes. Continue to contaminate your bed, and you will one night suffocate in your own waste. . . .

For our failure to thank you often for the wonders of creation, we ask forgiveness, Creator God.

Appendix A

The Youth Pledge
of Nonviolence

Student reflection on the seven components of the Pledge

Forgiveness

In chapter 8, activity 3, students reflected on the importance of forgiveness and how to put it into practice in their own lives.

The other six components

In the pages that follow, students are provided a series of questions that invite them to reflect on how they already have and have not put each component of the Pledge into practice, plus questions that challenge them to put it into practice more fully. Duplicate any or all of these pages and use them as you see fit.

Other resources on the Youth Pledge of Nonviolence

James McGinnis, *Alternatives to Violence Program Planning Guide and Teacher's Manual for Christian High Schools and Youth Groups*, Institute for Peace and Justice, 2003. A comprehensive 500-page guide for creating a school-wide program or a single course around the Youth Pledge of Nonviolence. It includes the material in *If Only Today You Knew . . . The Things That Make for Peace.*

James McGinnis, *If Only Today You Knew . . . The Things That Make for Peace—For High Schools and Youth Groups*, Institute for Peace and Justice, 2003. This unique 125-page resource for teachers and youth ministers on "peacemaking in post-9/11 America" challenges youth to put the gospel call to peace into practice.

James McGinnis, *A Call to Peace: 52 Meditations on the Family Pledge of Nonviolence*, Institute for Peace and Justice, 2000. A smaller inspirational and practical resource for living and teaching the Pledge of Nonviolence.

Website

Visit the website of the Institute for Peace and Justice (www.ipj-ppj.org) for a variety of other resources for living and teaching the Pledge of Nonviolence—essays, lessons plans, prayer services, and the complete catalog of Institute resources. You can order any of these resources online.

Newsletter on the Prison Pledge of Nonviolence

The Family Pledge of Nonviolence was adapted as a Prison Pledge by James McGinnis and the inmate facilitators of the Violent Offender Program at Missouri Eastern Correctional Center, where Jim works as a "volunteer in corrections." The men in the Violent Offender Program have been using the Pledge since 2000 as a way of reinforcing the positive way of living to which they have committed themselves. This special issue of the IPJ Newsletter includes an essay on each of the Pledge components by an inmate who committed to putting that component into practice long-term. These short essays, plus the process the men use in reflecting on the Pledge, are challenging and inspiring for youth and adults. Contact the Institute for Peace and Justice for a copy of this newsletter and duplicate and distribute it as you choose.

TO RESPECT SELF AND OTHERS

To respect myself, to affirm others and to avoid uncaring criticism, hateful words, physical or emotional attacks, negative peer pressure, and self-destructive behavior, including abuse of alcohol and drugs.

In terms of respecting myself—

➤ *Do I hang out with positive people or negative people? Why?*

➤ *In what ways have I given in to negative peer pressure? Why?*

➤ *Are there some changes I need to make in this area and what will be my first/next step?*

In terms of respecting others—

➤ *How have I engaged in uncaring criticism, hateful words, physical or emotional attacks? Why?*

➤ *What changes do I need to make in this area and what will be my first/next step?*

➤ *In what ways have I already been affirming of others?*

➤ *Is this easy or difficult for me to do? Why?*

➤ *What are some additional ways that I can be more affirming of others?*

➤ *What will be my next step in being a more affirming person?*

➤ *Who and what can help me follow through on any or all of these decisions?*

TO COMMUNICATE BETTER

To share my feelings honestly, to look for safe ways to express my anger and other emotions, to work at solving problems peacefully.

➤ *In what situations have I been dishonest about my feelings? Why?*

➤ *Are there some changes I need to make in this area and what will be my first/next step?*

➤ *In what situations have I handled my anger poorly? Why?*

➤ *In what situations do I tend to handle my anger positively? Why?*

➤ *Are there some changes I need to make in this area and what will be my first/next step?*

➤ *In what situations have I handled conflicts or problems poorly? Why?*

➤ *In what situations do I tend to handle conflicts or problems peacefully? Why?*

➤ *Are there some changes I need to make in this area and what will be my first/next step?*

➤ *Who and what can help me follow through on any of these changes?*

TO LISTEN

To listen carefully to others, especially those who disagree with me,
and to consider others' feelings and needs as valid as my own.

➤ *In what situations have I been a poor listener? Why?*

➤ *In what situations do I tend to listen carefully? Why?*

➤ *Are there some changes I need to make in this area and what will be my first/next step?*

➤ *In what situations have I ignored or discounted the feelings and needs of others? Why?*

➤ *In what situations do I tend to respond positively to the feelings and needs of others? Why?*

➤ *Are there some changes I need to make in this area and what will be my first/next step?*

➤ *Who and what can help me follow through on any or all of these changes?*

TO RESPECT NATURE

To live simply and value people more than things,
to treat the environment and all living things with respect and care,
and to promote environmental concern in our school.

➤ *In what ways do I consume more than my fair share of the earth's resources? Why?*

➤ *In what ways have I been more careful about what I consume and been more sharing with others? Why?*

➤ *Do I tend to value people more than things or things more than people? Why?*

➤ *Are there some changes I need to make in these areas and what will be my first/next step?*

➤ *What have I done to be wasteful and careless about the environment? Why?*

➤ *What have I done to be more careful about the environment? Why?*

➤ *Are there some changes I need to make in this area and what will be my first/next step?*

➤ *Who and what can help me follow through on any or all of these changes?*

To Recreate Nonviolently

*To select activities and entertainment that strengthen my commitment
to nonviolence and that promote a less violent society,
and to avoid social activities that make violence look exciting, funny or acceptable.*

➤ *How do I entertain myself in ways that glorify violence? Why do I enjoy them?*

➤ *In what ways have sports been a positive experience and/or a negative experience for me? Why?*

➤ *What effects do these activities have on my relationships with other people? On the kind of person I am becoming? Why?*

➤ *Do these activities make me more sensitive to violence or less sensitive? Why?*

➤ *What kinds of activities do I do that are more playful? That are more cooperative?*

➤ *What are some changes I need to make in this area? Why?*

➤ *What will be my first/next step in making these changes?*

➤ *Who and what can help me follow through on these changes?*

TO ACT COURAGEOUSLY

To actively challenge violence in all its forms whenever I encounter it, whether at home, at school, at work, or in the community, and to stand with others who are treated unfairly, even if it means standing alone.

➤ *What are some situations where I challenged violence or stood up for someone who was being treated unfairly? What were the results? How did it feel?*

➤ *What are some situations where I could have but didn't challenge violence or stand up for others? What were the results? How did it feel?*

➤ *Why is it often difficult to challenge violence and stand up for others?*

➤ *What are some changes I need to make in this area and what will be my first/next step?*

➤ *Who and what can help me follow through on these changes?*

Appendix B

Teens Acting for Peace (TAP) Program

A National Youth Violence Prevention Training Program

Introduction and Background

The Institute for Peace and Justice's Families Against Violence Advocacy Network (FAVAN) was launched in 1996 as a coalition of organizations, faith communities, local community groups, schools, and families. FAVAN's five-step strategy to provide alternatives to violence at all levels of human interaction begins with a Pledge of Nonviolence. To date, the Pledge has been translated into eighteen different languages and adapted for use in schools, workplaces, prisons, and faith communities. It has been embraced by more than 500,000 individuals and families and hundreds of schools and faith communities in the United States alone. Because of the effectiveness of peers in teaching nonviolence, the Teens Acting for Peace (TAP) Program was launched in 1999 to train teens to teach the Pledge to elementary-school-aged children.

Program Goals

1. To inspire and equip youth with the skills and values to make the Pledge of Nonviolence real in their interpersonal lives and to confront injustices and build peace in their communities.
2. To empower youth to teach children the skills and values embodied in the Pledge of Nonviolence, in school, after-school, and camp settings.
3. To challenge and help these youth leaders integrate the Pledge into their own schools and youth groups and encourage their families to make the Pledge a part of their family life.

Program Development

Catholic schools

TAP began as a pilot program in St. Louis in 1999. With funding from the Safe and Drug-Free Schools Program for Non-Public Schools, three Catholic high schools and ten elementary schools have participated in TAP. By the fourth year, the eighth-graders at three of the elementary schools were doing the presentations to the younger students at their own schools. In Kansas City, Kansas, and Kansas City, Missouri, TAP has expanded to four Catholic high schools and twelve elementary schools, plus one public high school. In Cincinnati, Ohio, two Catholic high schools have worked with five elementary schools.

Public schools

In Beaver, Baden, and Pittsburgh, Pennsylvania, the program began in 2000 as an after-school "Peace Camp," with Beaver public secondary and middle school youth teaching the Pledge in an elementary school in their district. Since 2002, college students and secondary school youth have been trained to conduct one-week summer peace camps in Baden and Pittsburgh, sponsored by the Sisters of St. Joseph. In 2000, 250 high school, middle school, and Job Corps youth and twenty adult advisors were trained in Grand Rapids, Michigan, where they work through the Institute for Global Education. In 2001, TAP was launched in the Tidewater, Virginia, area and the Outer Banks in North Carolina.

TAP Training and Resources

Goals for the Training Experience

1. Experience the Pledge. The training experience provides time for participants to experience and better understand the Pledge of Nonviolence.
2. Embrace the Pledge. The training experience invites and motivates participants to commit to putting the Pledge of Nonviolence into practice in their lives.
3. Energize to teach the Pledge. The training experience gives participants the confidence and energy they need to teach the Pledge to younger students.
4. Empower to transform. The training experience gives participants knowledge, skills, and a sense of hope that they can help to transform a part of their community, as well as their own lives.
5. Evaluate and improve the experience. The training experience gives participants the opportunity to evaluate the program and participate in its improvement.

Preferred training model—a two-day event

In twelve hours of training, the youth leaders and/or adult trainees experience all five of the training goals. They experience the full range of teaching methodologies applied to all seven components of the Pledge of Nonviolence; have time for reflecting on these methodologies, as well as on the content of the Pledge; experience each trainer's creativity, story, and the motivation that keeps them active; explore and share their own creativity and motivation; learn how to use the training resources for the program; explore what is appropriate for the grade levels which they will be teaching; and develop their own creative activities and present these to the other trainees for feedback.

Options

These two days can be back to back or at the beginning of each semester. When necessary, the event can be compacted into a six- or nine-hour program.

TAP Resources

These have included an *Adult Training Manual,* a *Youth Instructor Workbook,* and a *Lesson Plan Resource Book.* For information about their current availability, contact James McGinnis at jimppjn@aol.com or the online catalog of the Institute for Peace and Justice (www.ipj-ppj.org).

For more information on TAP training events and scheduling, contact James McGinnis at the Institute for Peace and Justice, 475 E. Lockwood, St. Louis, MO 63119; e-mail: jimppjn@aol.com. Also check the TAP web page on the website for the Institute for Peace and Justice: www.ipj-ppj.org. This TAP page also offers a description of the TAP Program and excerpts from the TAP resources.

Sources for Quotations

Chapter 1

Williamson, Marianne. *A Return to Love* (New York: HarperCollins, 1992).

The article "Then My Living Will Not Be in Vain," Ebenezer Baptist Church, February, 1968 is quoted from *A Testament of Hope: The Essential Writings and Speeches of Martin Luther King, Jr.*, James, Washington, ed. (San Francisco: HarperSanFrancisco, 1991), p. 267.

Chapter 2

The article "Babies in the River" was first used in James McGinnis, *Those Who Hunger* (New York: Paulist Press, 1979).

The article "Two Feet of Christian Service" was first used in James McGinnis, *Educating for Peace and Justice* (Institute for Peace and Justice, 1984).

Activity 3 and the student handout are adapted from more comprehensive treatments of Amos and the other Hebrew prophets in James McGinnis, *Teaching the Prophets; Living as Prophets* (Institute for Peace and Justice, 2004); and on the justice of Jesus in James McGinnis, *If Only Today You Knew: The Things That Make for Peace* (Institute for Peace and Justice, 2003).

"What Does the Lord Require?" music and lyrics are by Jim Strathdee from the *Jubilee* album (Jim and Jean Strathdee, Desert Flower Music, 1986). Contact Jim and Jean Strathdee at www.strathdee music.com.

Chapter 3

Pope Paul VI, *On the Development of Peoples*, 1967, #17 is quoted in *Renewing the Earth* (U.S. Catholic Bishops, 1991).

"A Christmas Sermon on Peace," December 24, 1967, is quoted from *A Testament of Hope: The Essential Writings and Speeches of Martin Luther King, Jr.*, p. 254.

Chapter 4

Prejean, Sr. Helen. *Dead Man Walking* (New York: Vintage Books, 1993), p. 37.

Bud Welch is quoted on the Journey of Hope website at www.journeyofhope.org. For more information on Bud Welch, see also: www.theforgivenessproject.com/stories/bud-welch.

Chapter 5

National Center for Injury Prevention and Control of the Centers for Disease Control and Prevention www.cdc.gov/ncipc/ncipchm.htm.

Chapter 6

"White Privilege" is adapted from Kathleen McGinnis, *Celebrating Racial Diversity* (Institute for Peace and Justice, 2005), p. 16.

"Racial Profile" is adapted from Kathleen McGinnis, *Celebrating Racial Diversity* (Institute for Peace and Justice, 2005), p. 16.

King, Martin Luther, Jr. *Stride Toward Freedom: The Montgomery Story* (New York: Harper, 1958), p. 205.

King, Martin Luther, Jr. *Why We Can't Wait* (New York: Signet Classic, 2000), pp. 109–110.

King, Martin Luther, Jr. *Where Do We Go From Here: Chaos or Community?* (New York: Harper, 1967), p. 93.

Ibid., p. 83.

"Letter from Birmingham Jail," quoted from *A Testament of Hope: The Essential Writings and Speeches of Martin Luther King, Jr.,* p. 292.

"A Christmas Sermon on Peace," December 24, 1967, is quoted from *A Testament of Hope: The Essential Writings and Speeches of Martin Luther King, Jr.,* pp. 257–258.

Chapter 7

"Jenny Boyce," is adapted from James McGinnis, *Educating for Peace and Justice* (Institute for Peace and Justice, 1993), p. 127–128.

Ferrell, Frank and Janet, *Trevor's Place* (Gladwyne, PA: Ferrell Family Endeavors, Inc.), p. 19 and p. 106.

"When Silence Is Betrayal," April 4, 1967, is quoted from *A Testament of Hope: The Essential Writings and Speeches of Martin Luther King, Jr.* p. 240.

This Land Is Home to Me, Part I, (Appalachian Catholic Bishops, 1975) pp. 17–18.

Carrigan, Ana. *Salvador Witness: The Life and Calling of Jean Donovan* (New York: Ballantine Books, 1984), p. 212

Romero, Archbishop Oscar, February 17, 1980, quoted in Jon Sobrino, *Archbishop Romero: Memories and Reflections* (Maryknoll, NY: Orbis Books, 1990), p. 38.

Romero, Archbishop Oscar, March 10, 1980, quoted in James Brockman, S.J., *The Word Remains: A Life of Oscar Romero* (Maryknoll, NY: Orbis Books, 1982), p. 223.

Chapter 8

Drawing of the "love/violence" scale was developed by Susan Crowe and reprinted with her permission.

U.S. Catholic Bishops. *The Challenge of Peace*, 1983, #327.

Ibid., #304.

King, Martin Luther, Jr., quoted in Vincent Harding, "Road to Redemption" (*The Other Side*, January/February 2003), p. 14.

The handout with the Amber Amundson letter is adapted from James McGinnis, *If Only Today You Knew The Things That Make for Peace* (Institute for Peace and Justice, 2003), p. AC 28.

"When Silence Is Betrayal," April 4, 1967, is quoted from *A Testament of Hope: The Essential Writings and Speeches of Martin Luther King, Jr.*, pp. 231, 240–242.

Chapter 9

Bouchard, Charles. "To Cross or Not to Cross: The Moral Dilemma of the Picket Line," *St. Louis Dispatch* (October 27, 2003). Reprinted with permission of the author.

Chapter 10

Austin, Richard. *Baptized into Wilderness: A Christian Perspective on John Muir* (Abingdon, VA: Creekside Press, 1991), p. 3.

Berry, Thomas. *The Dream of the Earth* (San Francisco: Sierra Club Books, 1988), pp. 42–43, 50–51.

Macy, Joanna Rogers. *Thinking Like A Mountain: Toward a Council of All Beings* (Santa Cruz, CA: New Society Publishers, 1988).

Thoreau, Henry David, quoted in Bradley Dean's Introduction to *Wild Fruits: Thoreau's Rediscovered Last Manuscript* (New York: WW Norton & Co., 2000).

Chief Black Elk, quoted in *The Sacred Pipe: Black Elk's Account of the Seven Rites of the Oglala Sioux* (Norman, OK: University of Oklahoma Press, 1953).

Chief Seattle, quoted in James McGinnis, *Bread and Justice: Toward a New International Economic Order* (New York: Paulist Press, 1979), pp. 322–323.

Dr. James McGinnis has over thirty years experience in writing curricula and leading workshops and retreats on peacemaking. He founded and works at the Institute for Peace and Justice in St. Louis.

Other Titles of Interest

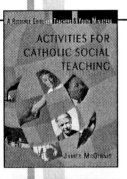

Activities for Catholic Social Teaching

A Resource Guide for Teachers and Youth Ministers

James McGinnis

A companion resource to *Catholic Social Teaching*, this workbook offers teenagers a chance to put into action the Church's body of social teaching. Consistent with the gospel message that action is an integral component of justice, each unit involves activities that motivate teens to act in a way that inspires change.

ISBN: 1-59471-067-8 / 224 pages / $19.95

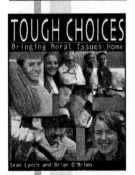

Revised!
Catholic Social Teaching

Learning and Living Justice

Michael Francis Pennock

Introduces high school students to issues surrounding the key principles of the Church's rich body of social teaching that comes to us from the strong tradition of the writings of the popes, especially since Pope Leo XIII. This textbook has been found in conformity with the *Catechism of the Catholic Church*.

STUDENT TEXT
ISBN: 1-59471-102-X / 288 pages / $22.95
TEACHER MANUAL
ISBN: 1-59471-103-8 / 288 pages / $26.95

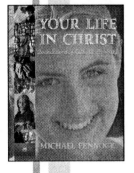

Tough Choices

Bringing Moral Issues Home

Sean Lynch & Brian O'Brien

A companion to *Your Life in Christ*, this resource for Catholic high schools and parish religious education provides ways for teenagers to learn and make choices about a number of current and practical moral issues. Some issues covered are: abortion, capital punishment, child abuse/domestic violence, divorce, drugs/alcohol, eating disorders euthanasia, homosexuality, sexuality, and suicide.

ISBN: 0-87793-993-4 / 192 pages / $16.95

Your Life in Christ

Foundations of Catholic Morality

Michael Pennock

Focuses on the essential message of Christ's moral teaching, the importance of love of God and love of neighbor, and presents it in a way that is clear and applicable to the lives of today's teenagers. This textbook has been found in conformity with the *Catechism of the Catholic Church*.

STUDENT TEXT
ISBN: 0-87793-949-7 / 288 pages/ $19.95
TEACHER MANUAL
ISBN: 0-87793-702-8 / 256 pages/ $26.95

Visit www.avemariapress.com for online resources for teachers and DRE's, as well as more information on the entire line of religion textbooks.

Available from **ave maria press**
Notre Dame, IN 46556 / www.avemariapress.com
ph: 1.800.282.1865 / fax: 1.800.282.5681
Prices and availability subject to change.

Keycode: F0A05060000

Printed in the United States
57424LVS00006B/135-512

9 781594 710674